fight like a mom
momswithcancer.org

> My dearest Carol
> I love you with all of my heart. Thank you for all of your support these many years. You are precious.
> I love You
> DeAnna

Fight Like a Mom
Copyright © 2012 by DeAnna Rice
PO Box 1442 Lake Forest, CA 92630
All rights reserved. No part of this book may be reproduced or transmitted in any form or by any means without written permission of the author.
ISBN: 978-0615703893

Dear God

Hear my prayers and answer them as you see fit.
I know you will never let me down.
Your plans for me are greater than I can ever imagine.

I promise to ...
never let worry consume me, walk with my head held high, to love as you have loved me, generously Dear God and abundantly.
To help when I can and when you speak to my heart (even if I can't understand or I am afraid).

I trust in you and am ready and open to make this world a better place because you made me.

Your Miracle
DeAnna

Dear Fellow Survivor,

I want you to know you are not alone. I want to share some thoughts and experiences with you that will hopefully guide you, answer questions, give you inspiration, and maybe even help calm your fear.

The number one thing I want you to take away from this book is my firm belief that getting cancer is NOT a death sentence. Many, many, many people not only survive this disease but they go on to lead fuller lives, filled with heightened meaning.

Nor is your life meant to be a death sentence. Some days may seem unbearable even when you aren't battling a disease. There are many ups and downs. I guarantee you that life is ever changing. My belief in God has helped me through the hardest times.

Now is the time to reacquaint yourself with you. With who you WANT to be. If there are changes you want to make, now is the perfect time. It's a time to delve into finding or throwing yourself into something you love. Whether it's a new career move, volunteering for an organization, advocacy, painting, boating, writing, making pottery, or scrapbooking. I urge you to try different things and find something that brings you pleasure and happiness. Your fears right now will undoubtedly be focused on your family, your children. Don't forget to take time to focus on what you LOVE to DO.

There are many stories we've heard, movies we've watched and possibly relatives we've watched deal with cancer. Let's face it, this is not a "normal" situation. Your family is watching you for cues as to how to act and feel. They need to know it's safe to continue to enjoy life. They need to see you having fun and enjoying life. There will be days when you will feel horrible. There will be days when you will be scared. These feelings are totally normal and to be expected. Acknowledge that it is okay. What you are feeling is okay.

I am here to share hope. I really understand the deepest of your fears. I have been there and survived five times. Yes, a BALD woman five times. YOU CAN DO THIS!!!!!!

Surviving and Thriving
DeAnna Rice

CONTENTS

Dear God		4
Dear Fellow Survivor		5
Contents		7
Acknowlegements		8
Introduction		12
Chapter 1:	My Memories	17
Chapter 2:	Opening Bell: The Bout Begins	33
Chapter 3:	They Knock You When You're Down	67
Chapter 4:	Round 2	83
Chapter 5:	Majority Decision – GO WEST!	110
Chapter 6:	Round 3	140
Chapter 7:	Round 4	165
Chapter 8:	Round 5	188
Chapter 9:	Unanimous Decision	192
Chapter 10:	Going the Distance-- 7 Steps to Happiness	194
My Scrapbook		203
About the Author		208
Tribute from Jordan		209
Glossary		210

Acknowledgements

Writing this book has been a difficult and long process. Timing is everything. This book would not be what it is today if I had attempted to write this a mere four years ago. In those four years my life has turned around. Because of a doctor who was so committed to treating cancer, a doctor who wasn't yet my doctor; a doctor who took the time to listen to my story of cancer, and being wise enough to unleash on me like a pit bull. To Dr. Lisa Curcio, I owe my life. Thank you for educating as many people as you can reach. It is my honor to call you a friend.

I also want to thank the other team of doctors who have treated me and kept me alive through all of my cancers and heart failure. Dr. Jeb Brown, you have been a shining light that has believed in my strength to beat each of my cancers. Thank you. Dr. Bruss, you have worked with me yearly to rebuild my heart, compassionately feeling the sorrow of each of my cancers. Thank you. It has been a long haul and I appreciate each of you for all you have done.

In this section I need to recognize the doctors and healthcare professionals who treated me poorly--like a number. They did not take the time to see me as a person, a mom, a wife, a daughter, a sister, a friend. These are the individuals that made insensitive comments. Its one thing to endure insensitivity from the general public. It's quite another to be treated this way by a "professional" working in healthcare as their chosen field. Some of these individuals were downright rude, almost to the point of being cruel. I hope no one you know personally is ever treated the way you treated me. This is all the space I will devote to you.

To Todd and Tim: I have been blessed twice with husbands who are truly "stand-up-and-be-counted-on" loving men. The first one was lost as a result of decisions I made poorly, and out of fear. The second, I was lucky enough to have as a friend and grew to love me for me, faults and all. Even when one of the doctors couldn't believe that you married me "even though I had all of the problems."

I treasure both of you and appreciate the encouragement and support you have given me over the years.

My kids:
Raquel: my little angel; the little girl who

grew up too fast trying to make up for my illnesses and being a caretaker. Raquel you are the one who gave up so much happiness to be troubled so deeply by having a Mom who was sick so often. You are a blessing and I hope someday you will understand how incredible I think you are, and how much I believe in you.

Jordan: my little funny man. Somehow you were always able to make me laugh with your silly antics. You are a sensitive guy and oh so tough-looking to the outside world. I hope people take the time to look into your heart and recognize the fears you felt growing up. My hope for you is to realize your potential, and make the difference in this lifetime that I know you are searching to make.

Phillip: My baby. What can I say? You have always been a blessing. My heart loved you so deeply from the first time I knew you were here. You are a special young man. Much like your brother and sister, you have had to endure way too much. I adore you and love you.

Taylor: my surprise. You were meant to be here, despite the terror I felt when I knew you were coming to me. It wasn't until I looked at you and knew that it was YOU, my Taylor, that I was captivated and awed by God's miracle in placing you as my child.

My children... I am sorry you have had to endure all of this. But, I am so happy to be your Mom. I have learned a lot along the way and unfortunately I had to learn "on the job." But you are each amazing people, I'm proud of you, and I love you so much.

I have also been blessed by four other children as a result of marriage. -Lauren my first non-birthed child. Laura, Karen and Shannon, the three of you have added to my joy and have truly completed the puzzle of my life. Thank you for accepting me and allowing me to love your Dad.

Introduction

Today is a day filled with so many emotions. I cannot begin to explain what they mean or even how to deal with them. It is my son Phillip's graduation day. 18 years ago when he was a seven-month-old baby, I was diagnosed with breast cancer. I was told if I made it five years, I could take a breath. Today, I sit in the stands in the auditorium of Dominion High School watching him receive his diploma. I am sitting with his Dad and I can barely control my tears.

I quickly think back to where the past 18 years have taken all of us. Many years filled with joy, many others filled with pain and heartbreak. Today is a sign that we have made it. Through the good and the bad, I am alive and I have been able to see our son graduate high school.

This book will take you through my ups and downs. I have bared my soul. It was painful for me to relive the downs of my life. The gain will be worth the pain, if I can help one person understand that their past does not dictate their future. The game is never over until you quit. Every day is a fresh start no matter how horrible the last day was. I am embarrassed by my history; if I could change it I would. I can't. So over the years I have learned to accept it, and learn from it. The most difficult part was acknowledging that this, in fact, WAS my life. I am judged by it and assumptions have been made about me. For many decades I have not told the entire story.

By the grace of God, I am able to share my story with you. I accept my life's condition. It is what it is. I take seriously my responsibility to get to every person and reach as many people as possible and give them information that can change their lives, like it did mine.

Parts of this book are straight out of my journal. You will note those as they are very specific and written in italics. Please remember that I am but a girl diagnosed with cancer. I have been scared. I have made bad decisions. Thank you for reading and listening to my story of hope.

In my dreams, I hope the story of my life is able to inspire you through whatever journey you are going through. We all learn life's lessons in our own way. However, no one said that we have to do it alone, nor did they say we have to reinvent the wheel. Learn from my challenges. You are not alone.

Hereditary Cancers
As we (men and women) age, we have a higher risk of developing cancer. Factors that are significant are familial factor, an environmental factor, or heredity. Our chances naturally go up with age. It is increasingly more important to follow the recommendations for diet and exercise that will keep these chances from skyrocketing.

For hereditary breast and ovarian cancer patients carrying the BRCA genetic mutation, our risk as women goes up to the 90th percentile that we will develop cancer in our lifetime. It is a staggering statistic. For the majority of us carriers, this means that unless we die from an accident or other means before we are diagnosed with cancer, it will be the only way to avoid the diagnosis. To have any chance of survival, we must be tested and educated about early detection and risk reducing measures.

The number of people diagnosed with a genetic mutation is relatively low for the general population. But for those of us carrying a mutation, just knowing that you are a carrier is the key to life. When identified early, this knowledge gives us the power to avoid developing that first, second, third or more cancers in our lifetime.

Genetic testing that identifies the presence of a mutation is often life saving. It gives us the information we need to be medically managed correctly. There are appropriate specific criteria that would indicate whether a patient is at risk. So, not all people should rush out and demand this test be given to them.

The specific gene mutation I am affected with has been identified as the BRCA1 mutation. BRCA stands for breast and ovarian cancer. The BRCA test is for women who have been diagnosed with breast cancer before the age of fifty, women who have been diagnosed with ovarian cancer at ANY age, or men who have had breast cancer at any age. This is also true for first, second, and third degree relatives. If your family has a positive history of cancer that is striking, meaning more than one diagnosis with at least one being under age 50 for breast cancer, you should strongly look into this test. There are numerous genetics tests that are being offered at the time of this writing.

Typically the family history tells the story, but that is not always the case. In my case, my paternal grandmother had breast cancer in her 40's and passed away at 52 from metastatic breast cancer to her brain. But, the most obvious and glaring, part of my story that should have been a red flag-was my diagnosis with breast cancer at 29 years of age.

Chapter 1: My Memories

Born in Long Beach, CA, I grew up as a happy, normal child during my first 6 years. I don't remember anything negative. I remember being loved. My family and extended family played an important part of my life. They were always around. Extended cousins galore, uncles and aunts. Two sets of Grandparents and of course, my Mom Linda, and Dad Larry, and my little brother Shannon.

My deep belief in God and love for Jesus started with my paternal Grandma, LaVerne Howe. From the time I was very young, every Sunday she would dress me up in a beautiful dress. All of her friends would ohhh and ahhhh at my pretty dress, my red hair, and shy smile.

This is a book about God and how I am here to serve. It's about my journey through many difficult times and about living with choices that I have made. The biggest part of my story is no matter what has happened, God's love for me has endured. There were times when I couldn't stand to look at myself in the mirror. At times when I didn't know how I could take another breath and face my future, I always knew deep down, somehow God had a plan for me.

As a child, I always felt special and loved. From a young age, before I have any real memories, I remember loving God. As a child, I always thought that I was in a play. God was the director, and everyone else was an actor in my life. I remember being about eight when I made that analogy. I was riding in the back of a pick-up truck, lost in my own thoughts, already thinking about my life. I felt special, like there was a plan. I had a destiny. Never could I imagine the life that was about to unfold before me.

My parents were very young when they found out they were expecting me. My Mom was only 16 and my Dad was 18. My Moms parents, The Grijalva's, made it very clear they were not happy about the "situation" and did not support the family we were forced to become. I was never allowed to stay the night at their house, and my Grandma Grijalva never babysat me. In fact, I remember growing up hearing her tell my Mom "You made your bed, now you lie in it." Words that would come back to haunt me many years later.

My Dad's parents were quite the opposite. The Howe's were loving and fun. My Grandma Howe was sick quite often. At a time when it wasn't spoken about, she was diagnosed with breast cancer at a very young age. She endured a double mastectomy and hysterectomy. Things were different in the sixties, she had no reconstruction and she didn't do chemotherapy. The breasts were gone, therefore the cancer was gone.

As a young child, we moved in with my paternal grandparents. I can still remember the homey smell of their house. It was a combination of vitamins (my grandpa was a health nut) and chicken cooking. It seems there was always something on the stove. My memories are filled with love and laughter in their home. My Grandpa, George Howe was a silly man. He worked hard his entire life and made a good life for his family. He bought a quaint little home in Long Beach, California where all of the yards were perfectly manicured. He used to use our heads and pretend they were a gear shifter. First gear up…..rrrrrrrrr….second gear down…….rrrrrrrrrr…..third gear up and to the right…….. OH NO a stop!. Screech! Eeerrrrrkkkkk. We would laugh so hard and scream "Again, again!!"

Grandpa Howe loved his electronics. I thought we lived in a Jetson's house. He had intercoms and speakers piped through the entire house. Music or more often we would hear him teasing us. "Hound dogs????? I'm gonna get you!" Again he had us laughing.

My Mom didn't care for my Grandma Howe or maybe it started the other way around. Either way there was constant tension and bickering between the two of them. Even when we moved out and lived in our own place we were often at their home for dinners, croquet games in the backyard, or just being babysat. My Dad's family and extended family gave us the true meaning of family. Not long after my Dad's extended family moved out to the country in the Antelope Valley. We moved to be closer to them. My Dad couldn't believe we could find such a nice home on an acre of land on a tree lined street in a friendly farm community called Littlerock, CA. for only $19,900.

Aunt Tenie, Grandma Grijalva and Mom

The Grijalva grandparents were different. I always had a pretty close relationship with them, but it was very different than that of the Howe grandparents. My Grandpa, William Grijalva, was a quiet hard working man. When the weekends rolled around he would allow himself the reward of beer. It was during those times that his personality showed. He was actually very funny and loving. Without alcohol, he was quiet and loved his old Jalopy cars he raced. When he was alone with Shannon and me, he would tell us stories and try to teach us Spanish. He was born in Los Angeles, but I'm not really too sure how much he knew himself. I never met any of his family. When he married my Grandma he was disowned. They met when he was in the military, and she drove a truck to the military bases to deliver supplies. Grandma Grijalva had a hard life. She had a second grade education, but she was street smart. She was sassy and blunt.

When I was a teenager, she and I became much closer. I was having a very hard time and would call her for advice and begged her to let me finish High School, living with her. During those times she confided in me and told me stories of her prior early life and suddenly I understood so much more about her. She had two children prior to my Mom and her sister Christine. She had been raped and molested as a child. She married young to make her own life--only to have married an alcoholic. They divorced and she was raising the two children, a boy and a girl, alone.

When her first two children were young, Grandma Grijalva became very ill and wasn't expected to live through a surgery. She was told if she died, her children would become wards of the state and go separately into an orphanage. However, she could sign them over and they would be kept together and be adopted together…if she died. She signed the papers, had the surgery and unexpectedly lived! Her children were still not allowed to come back home. They were adopted out together and many years later they came and met her. But when those children were taken, I believe a part of her soul died. My Grandma was notoriously crotchety. It was not until she told me this heart-breaking story, that I began to understand her. I actually developed a great deal of compassion for her.

My Dad

My Dad, Larry, was living the fast life as a Hollywood stuntman. It seemed he was forever back and forth living between our house and elsewhere. As soon as I started High School he left for good. My brother, Shannon, shared his wanderlust and soon left to live with him. I didn't speak to my Dad for probably 3 years. I watched my

Mom go from being funny to being a hurt,

bitter person. I couldn't blame her. It was now more difficult to feel close to her. She put up a wall that I couldn't penetrate. The pain she endured made me very angry at my Dad.

As a Freshman in High School, we were financially struggling. I was watching my Mom work three jobs. I worked one job through a school work program. We were barely making ends meet, so I, reluctantly decided that I would sell my very precious horse, "Peaches" and give my Mom the money. That would save us from buying feed and hay every week.

I got Peaches for Christmas 5 years earlier. It is a memory I will always cherish. My parents told my brother Shannon and me that it had snowed outside. We had already finished opening all of our presents and they kept shouting, "It's snowing, it's snowing. Come look!" Shannon and I both ran to the back patio. We looked outside and all I could see was a beautiful red horse with white spots on her rump, looking at me. Time stopped. I stopped. I was confused. I was looking for snow. I could hear Shannon screaming too. I looked at my parents and they said, "Well, go on. She's yours." I went up to her and stuck my face into her long neck and

hugged her as hard and as long as I could.

I couldn't believe Shannon was as excited over this beautiful creature as I was. I looked over at him and he was jumping up and down in front of his new motorcycle. I didn't even see it. When I looked outside for that snow, all I could see was "Peaches". For the next 5 years she was my best friend. She was my sanity. When our family was falling apart, I could always count on my horse. I would bridle her up, hop on her bareback, and we would ride. We would be gone for hours. No one cared. I was safe in our little community, riding through the foothills, and up and down the creek bed, I could think and I could dream. Every penny I earned through babysitting and my jobs, I spent on her. I saved up enough to buy a hot pink halter and bareback pad. "Peaches" was my pride and my joy.

My Peaches

Deciding to sell "Peaches" was the hardest thing I've ever had to do. I can't tell you how many tears I cried. It was also the beginning of depression and loneliness that would plague me most of my life.

I felt safe selling "Peaches" to a woman I knew. She worked as my Dad's agent for a while, when he was acting and doing stunt work. She had agreed to make payments to me. Being a trusting 13 year old, who respected adults, I believed her. She took my horse and I never saw one payment. I was so scared to tell my Mom what happened! I looked for her and that beautiful horse for years. I was so mad, cheated, and felt so betrayed!

My Mom

My mom has so many qualities I would love to have. She is probably the most creative and funny person I know. She is terribly quick-witted. Wickedly quick-witted. If I ever needed help with writing an advertisement, I know I could always call her. I guess, as a daughter the thing I always wanted from her was acceptance, and for her to love me. I may sound a bit dramatic, but I guess I wanted to be treasured by her.

Suckerpunched!

For as long as I could remember, as a pre-teen girl, I had a mad crush on a boy, let's call him Steven. I remember all through junior high being so enamored with him. In sixth grade my best friend Gina and I would round the corner in the school hall and he would be standing there. All I could do was stop. He would walk by and we would giggle until we fell down.

As High School approached, my crush never stopped. He was even cuter then. We all belonged to a small archery club in our community. I got to know Steven better. As a group, we would go camping. I was smitten. He picked me up from my house and took me to school. We didn't have a boyfriend/girlfriend relationship. I was far too shy to have a boyfriend. We remained friends and continued to be flirty and giggle. For me it was perfect.

The weekend of my sixteenth birthday, our group was participating in an archery tournament in Las Vegas. My Mom, Steven and I drove out together. We watched our club members compete and then caught a show to celebrate my birthday. That evening began so fun. We saw Bill Cosby and Natalie Cole in concert. We had a photo taken of the three of us and we were all smiles.

Somehow during the evening out, things changed and comments from my Mom became snarky. I don't even remember what I was being teased about. But, I was embarrassed. I grabbed a blanket and a towel, locked myself in the hotel bathroom, and cried myself to sleep. Everything in my life changed that night.

Shortly after we returned home, Steven and my Mom were sneaking around. By the time I started my junior year, Steven had graduated from High School and had moved into our house. I was humiliated, betrayed, and heartbroken on so many levels. I had no one. At school the kids who knew what was going on in my household, teased me mercilessly. Which was pretty much everyone. I just needed out. I started dating a guy that got me out of the house. He was arrogant and a jerk. He always thought he was better than me and he let me know it.

All I knew was that my Mom was happy to have me out of the house, and I was just as happy to be gone. The tensions were high and this is when I started calling my Grandma Grijalva. She was sympathetic, but there was no way I could move in with her.

Luckily for me, I had accumulated so many credits through work experience and taking extra college classes, that my school counselor called me in. She told me that I had more than enough credits to graduate. I added the final government class to my schedule and graduated high school one year early.

I attended community college but my main thoughts were on getting out of my Mom's house. I spent as much time at my boyfriend's house that I could, and I was rarely home. I came home one day to find boxes of my things piled on the front porch for me. The relationship between my Mom and I had dwindled into a pile of nothing but disgust, jealousy and disrespect.

Just after high school I reconnected with my Dad. He had moved to Northern California and we had driven up to see him. I was so happy to be around him again. Granted, he was a self-admitted, crappy Dad when I was young, but having apologized on many occasions, I knew he loved me. Beyond that, I knew he liked me as a person.

My Dad and his girlfriend, Dawn, and Shannon moved back to Southern California and opened a stunt driving school with his best friend Speed Stearns. I spent as much time with them and their (to me) dysfunctional way of living. But hey, it worked for them, and they were having fun. They were working on movies and I got to do some photography on the set.

Abuse was a normal thing at my boyfriend's house. There was an unspoken code. I remember one time his dad attacked us with a chain while we were driving away in his truck. Why I didn't escape then, I can only attribute to me having the lowest self-esteem on the planet.

A year after I graduated high school, I became pregnant. I had never felt such joy. I was so happy that finally I would have someone to love forever. I vowed to be the best Mom and to never hurt my child the way I had been hurt.

After I had my beautiful baby, the abuse in our household kicked in full force. The first time I was hurt was when Raquel was only a month or so old. I was held down with his hand across my throat while he choked me. I was in shock. As much of a jerk as he was, he had never hurt me. It continued to get worse. I was thrown against walls. I was strangled to the point of passing out. Every time I tried to leave he would threaten me. He would kill me when he found me. This went on and off for a long time. If he suspected I was going to leave he would tell me that he would find me and he would start with my Mom and systematically kill everyone until he got to me.

There were times when I would be hiding and he would follow me and find me. One time he got me into his car. I had Raquel on my lap and he took out a gun and held it to my head and told me he was going to kill me right then. I begged and pleaded. I promised him I would never leave and I would go home. This cycle went on for years. I would leave, he would break into my place, threaten me and strangle me, and I would promise to come back. It was a violent and ugly situation. I tried to make it work. It was embarrassing to admit failure. I became pregnant with my second child, Jordan but I just couldn't do it anymore. I was depressed and I was scared.

I finally sought counseling at the domestic

violence shelter. I was too afraid to leave him and stay there, but I went in for counseling and slowly pulled my life back together. I continued to go to school, driving all the way to Pasadena City College for television production classes. I applied for a job at the local cable station selling advertising, so I could produce commercials. I finally made the move and left forever.

It took many years for him to stop following me around town. I just had to believe that he would never act on his threats at this point. I was still petrified. I even found him going through our garbage after we moved to Virginia. To this day I have to sleep with the TV on at night and have fleeting thoughts of being killed by him.

While working at the cable station in 1988 I began to rebuild my life. I made friends. Suzanne and Natalie became a safe haven of laughter and good times while at work. I met Todd there and we married shortly after. I finally found happiness. It took me years to behave like a normal thinking person. I pretended very well. I started hosting the radio show. I worked on several television pilots in Los Angeles and then in 1993, I got pregnant with Phillip. My life was complete. I was happy.

Chapter 2
The Opening Bell: The Bout Begins

My Perfect Life Blows Up

It was December 1994. Todd and I were getting ready to celebrate our anniversary in a few days. We had three beautiful children, Phillip, seven months, Jordan, seven-years-old and Raquel eleven.

Just before Ddagnosis

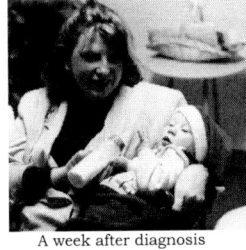
A week after diagnosis

Raquel and Jordan

At Todd's insistence, I had reluctantly gone to see the doctor. I had felt a lump in my left breast and it was rapidly growing. Months earlier, I questioned my OB about it and she replied, "It's probably just a swollen milk duct, it will go away when you're done breastfeeding." Just like that, it was dismissed. And just like that, I let it go. After all, I was only 29. I was healthy and had just had a baby by c-section. I was under the watchful eye of a doctor for nine months.

It wasn't until my lump could be grabbed and held onto, that it became a daily topic between us. Even then, I wasn't concerned. Todd harassed me about going to the doctor and having it checked. I thought he was being silly. I told him what the doctor had said and I was still nursing my baby, Phillip. But Todd was relentless. "Please just have it checked." he pushed for days.

Dramatically, I dialed my primary care doctors' number. "Hi...my husband wants me to come in and have a lump checked." I said. "I'm sure it's nothing, but he's really bugging me." They made the appointment, he was content.

Missed Cues

In 1992, a couple of years earlier, I had felt something and brought it to the attention of Carol, my nurse practitioner. I was only 27 and I was too young to worry about it. I just had lumpy dense breasts, which was a totally normal condition. She wasn't concerned, so neither was I. I went on living my life and continuing to concentrate on my perfect family and creating our perfect life.

Coincidentally, when I went in to have my lump checked in 1993, it was Carol the same nurse practitioner that I saw for my check up. I explained to her that I had asked my obstetrician about the lump and

I was told it was probably just a swollen milk duct. If it became infected or painful she would call in an antibiotic for me.

I took Carol's hand and placed it on my breast lump, "Here, feel." I said.

I showed her that I could actually grab it and she immediately told me she would be right back. I waited. It seemed like it took her forever. I just figured she needed to finish up with some other patient. When she walked back into the room, I looked into her eyes and I knew something was wrong. She wanted me to see Dr. Gerald Brouwer, the surgeon, let him check it, and see what he thought. Maybe it was a milk duct that was infected. We'll let him decide. The plan was for the office staff to call me when an appointment was set up. I remember this was on Tuesday, December 6th in the afternoon. I figured if I had heard anything by the end of the week I'd be lucky.

An hour after I got home, I got the phone call that Dr. Brouwer would see me the next day. I was petrified. I had a fear of needles that was immense. Not a normal fear, but an extreme, irrational fear that made me want to vomit, I would cry at the mere thought of being punctured by a needle. Now he wanted to stick a large needle into my breast. My breast that was full of milk to feed my baby!

Wednesday, December 7th, I walked into the appointment that would change my life. Todd came in and held my hand. The doctor would do a fine needle biopsy, and see if he could identify this as a cyst. He froze the area with a numbing spray and he proceeded to insert the needle into the hard mass of tissue. He pulled on the syringe. Nothing. He withdrew the needle and reinserted it. Again nothing. I closed my eyes and have no idea how many times he actually did this. He told me that he couldn't get anything from the aspiration. Dr. Brouwer wanted to go in and remove the lump; cut it out. He said he didn't know what it was, but he wanted it out. "What?" I couldn't grasp what he was telling me. He stepped out to get it set up. When he came back, he said they scheduled it for Friday morning. The next day I needed to go over to the hospital to have a pre-operative exam.

I had a chest x-ray, and blood tests were done. I signed admittance and insurance papers. They were going to biopsy the lump and it would be a simple outpatient procedure. I had just enough time to call Phillip's babysitter to come and sit with him during my surgery She was my best friend Sharmane's grandmother, Madear. Our older children, Raquel and Jordan, would be in school. I would be done and home before they got home.

I was calm the day of the surgery. Early in the morning on December 9th, Todd and I went to Lancaster Community Hospital and were escorted back to the outpatient area. A few years ago, I worked at this hospital and I was comfortable here. I changed into my gown and waited. I knew it would be fine. I just felt everything was going to be okay. I jokingly told him that if I had cancer, I would have lost weight and be thin, which I certainly wasn't.

The anesthesiologist introduced himself to me and it was only seconds before I was out. I woke up to Todd's face looking into mine. I struggled to focus on his face. I asked him "How'd it go?" He had tears running down his face and said words I'll never forget. "Not good sweetie." I fell back into my drugged anesthetized state.

"Mrs. Post, we need you to sit up. Are you awake, Mrs. Post?" The recovery room nurse was rubbing my arm and waking me up. I was able to sit up and she put me into a wheelchair. She leaned down close to my face, with her hands gripping the arms of the wheelchair. She looked into my eyes and said, "Fight this. DeAnna, you have to fight this." A million thoughts were running through my head. I had no idea what she was talking about. I had no clue.

I walked into the house and saw the light flashing on our answering machine. As always, I walked over and pressed the button. "Hi DeAnna. I'm sorry I just heard. If you need anything, please call". The next one and the one after that said the same thing.

I knew what the nurses, Todd, and my well-wishing friends were talking about, but no one had said the "C" word to me. Dr. Brouwer had told Todd that I had breast cancer. They had done a biopsy called a frozen section while I was in surgery. It was malignant. My Mom was in the hospital waiting room, and so were my friends, Sue and Becky. The doctor broke the news to them all together. He said it was bad. He wanted me back in the following week for a double mastectomy. He <u>never told me</u>. No one at the hospital talked to me about what the plan was.

I remember waking up at home in my bed and it was dark. I could hear Todd playing with Phillip in the family room. I was so tired. All I could do was get up and say "Hi" and go back to bed. Raquel and Jordan were already in bed asleep.

Suddenly, I sat up in bed. I'm not sure what time it was. It must have been three or four in the morning on Saturday, December 10th. I was finally clear-headed enough to process what was happening. I had Cancer! I had to just sit there by myself and digest this. It was too early to do anything. It was before the days of having a computer accessible to do a Google search for "cancer". I just waited. The sun rose and I woke up every hour until it was late enough to make a phone call.

I was the host of a talk radio show in the Antelope Valley. It wasn't a "reality" show…there was no yelling, no fighting, it was all about making our lives better. For over 5 years, I had been interviewing people about different topics. I loved that job. I was inquisitive, and loved interviewing people. I have always been intrigued by people's stories. It's fascinating to find out how they got where they are, why they think the way they do. Months before, I had interviewed a special lady, Ruth Mendoza, from the Ladies of Courage, a local breast cancer support group. I carefully dialed her number at around 8:20 A.M. a respectable and acceptable time to make a phone call.

I could hear someone crying. It was me. I carefully explained to her the events of the past couple of days. "I have breast cancer". It was the first time I said the words out loud. She began asking me a series of questions. I had no answers. I didn't know anything. She told me to get a pen and start keeping notes of every conversation I had from that moment on. "Don't trust your memory," she said. "Always write it down, or better yet, tape record every conversation and appointment". Soon, she was at my front door with a bag of brochures and papers.

Becoming My Own Advocate

Todd's mom, Dixie, is a nurse and a cancer survivor. She began working with Todd from the time I was diagnosed. She had spent that first evening of my diagnosis researching and making phone calls. She recommended we get the newly released book by Dr. Susan Love. Todd and I loaded up the kids and headed to the mall in search of "Dr. Love's Breast Book".

As soon as I started getting information, I felt more in control. All of a sudden, I went from victim to advocate for myself. The breast book was too much information to process in such a short period of time. I needed to start off slower. I talked to Todd's mom. Dixie told me about multidisciplinary cancer programs. How lucky we were to live in Southern California. We had top medical facilities.

top doctors and top schools. The two that came out with great cancer programs were UCLA and USC. But before I could contact them, I had to get more information. It would have to wait until Monday--only three short days from my scheduled surgery date--but it felt like a lifetime. This was the beginning of me learning patience, how to calm myself and truly understand that God was going to be a rock for me to get through all of this. All I could do was read, and try to keep all of us from becoming panicked.

Monday morning came and I started calling Dr. Brouwer. I called every hour. All day went by--I received no return call. I had waited long enough. I drove to his office and spoke to his wife who was the office manager. She told me he wasn't in the office. The fear that had built up inside of me all weekend, coupled with the fact that I had not heard from him for three long days, took its toll on me. I could no longer accept second hand information. I needed answers badly. I demanded to know what was going on. I wanted to talk to him, NOW. She got him on the phone and explained to him that I was very upset, and I really needed to talk to him.

As Ruth Mendoza recommended, I grabbed the closest piece of paper and a pen, and took notes on what he said to me. "You are the first patient in 20 years to question me about your treatment." I was furious. Again, as if to solidify my role, there was a palpable transformation from victim to advocate. All day I waited to just talk to him. He never had the courtesy to call me back—first to tell me that I had cancer, let alone tell me that he planned a double mastectomy as his preferred treatment. All I knew was what Todd had relayed to me. I continued to press him for this much-needed information. I have a fairly aggressive malignant unknown type of breast cancer. He proceeded to tell me that he was a specialist and he had done over a thousand procedures on women with breast cancer. I still have that handwritten note. It serves as a reminder of the moment I became my own advocate.

The Struggle for Information

I left there being very upset and went directly to my primary care doctor's office. Dr. Arul was the director of the medical group. Fortunately, I served on a Child Abuse Prevention Board with him. Maybe it would spur him to be compassionate with me. He brought me into his office. I explained to him what had just happened. He assured me that whatever I needed, I would get. My job was to fight. True to his word, I never had to argue for anything that I needed.

It would have taken a short conversation with Dr. Brouwer to reassure me what was happening. I got nothing from him. I knew that I could never trust this insensitive surgeon to operate on me again. I was also sure I didn't want to rush into the suggested mastectomy until I had all of the facts. So, I was off to get those facts. I was fueled by watching my grandmother's mastectomies, and how it affected her mentally and physically.

The two places that kept standing out for breast cancer treatment were UCLA and USC. Dr. Susan Love worked with UCLA. Ruth went to USC for treatment. My dream was to graduate from UCLA and I was taking extension courses to reach that goal. I loved everything about UCLA. I loved West LA, Beverly Hills… the smell of the jasmine flowers that permeated the city. I figured Dr. Love was there, besides, the shopping and food in this beautiful area were way better! I could at least get a degree of life through all of this from my beloved UCLA. (Shallow me…you'll learn more about that later!) I had to choose UCLA for each and every one of the reasons I described above.

I called the multidisciplinary coordinators office and they set up an appointment for later in the week for Friday, December 16, 1994. We would be meeting with an entire team of doctors: surgeon, oncologist, radiologist, psychiatrist and nursing coordinator. They needed all of my information 24 hours prior to the appointment. I ran all over town getting copies of my pathology reports, biopsy slides, chart history, and the surgeon's report.

New Team Steps In

The next day was Thursday, December 15, 1994, our wedding anniversary. Phillip and I drove an hour-and-a-half to UCLA to hand deliver all of the information they needed for my appointment. I had to do some more blood tests while I was there. Phillip and I rushed back to get ready for a family dinner to celebrate our anniversary. It gave us a sense of normalcy…at least for a couple of hours. But every time I looked at Todd, I felt his pain. He looked nauseated. The funny thing is, I felt okay. In this short period of time my confidence had grown. I knew I was accomplishing something, and I felt in control. I wouldn't have switched places with him in a million years.

December 16th, 1994
What a great day. We met Dr. Susan Love.

She's actually going to be my doctor. I have a stage 2 cancer. They want to do 6 months of chemo and 7 weeks, 5 days a week of radiation therapy. I asked them about the double mastectomy I was scheduled to have. I was told they no longer cut off women's breasts because of cancer. Dr. Love said statistically there is nothing that says that a mastectomy is anymore effective than a lumpectomy. Breast conservation. I'll have another surgery in January to check my lymph nodes and the area where the tumor was, to make sure the margins are clear.

We met the oncologist, Dr. Linnea Chap. What a great team I have. I'm very confident with everyone. They said my prognosis was excellent. I knew it already. Todd looks better. Hearing it from them made him feel better. Can you believe it's only been a week? It feels like a lifetime. I feel great.

When we went to the appointment, they had a few questionnaires for me to fill out. Family history, work exposure, environmental exposure, etc. My Dad's mom had breast cancer that had metastasized to her brain. She died when I was in 4th grade. I believe she was in her early 50's. I was told that there was no link from a paternal grandparent for breast cancer, another missed cue. I still had no answer as to why I had this huge tumor that was growing in my breast at 29 years old.

The team decided that being very aggressive was the only way to go. The cancer was aggressive and we needed to attack it aggressively. My age concerned them, so in that respect I know I'm going to kill any rogue cells that MAY be floating around. I will lose my hair. I will be bald. All I know of chemo is what I've seen on TV. The movie "Dying Young" depicted it as a horrible experience and that's all I know. I didn't yet personally know anyone who has had chemotherapy.

My surgery is scheduled for January 3, 1995. Happy New Year!

In preparation for my surgery, I had my first mammogram. My stitches were still in, and my breasts were still filled with milk. The compression from the machine popped my stitches open, and I was leaking from the open wound. That was an experience I could have done without.

It's funny, my cancer had women all over town checking their breasts. It scared them that a healthy, 29-year-old could be diagnosed with breast cancer. I had become a member of a club I never wanted to join. Pink will never be an ordinary color for me. I did get a call from Carol, my nurse practitioner, early one morning. She told me how upset she was, and how she couldn't eat, and now she would never take any chances. She'll be sending everyone who presents with a lump, to do a mammogram or send them to a surgeon for a consultation. I'm thankful she called. I felt my first victory as an advocate for another family.

Todd's mom, Dixie came into town. She was a rock. Her nursing career had guided us well over the past week. We were going to have some fun with her and the kids. Disneyland and the works!

Only a week and a half after my original surgery, we headed off for Disneyland. The happiest place on earth turned into a nightmare for me. My incision site became infected. I spiked a high fever. I could barely walk. We called the doctors office and they called in an antibiotic. Todd took me back to the hotel where he stayed by my side, and I slept the rest of the day.

Another Scare

We made it through Todd's birthday and Christmas. Everything went well. I did learn that 50% of all breast cancer occurs in the upper outer quadrant of the breast, exactly where mine was. It makes me question why I was not diagnosed earlier.

How did I just go through a pregnancy and never have my breasts examined? Even when *I* brought it up, it was dismissed and left unchecked. I can't help wonder about the "if only". Anger was sneaking in.

Caring for the kids and working was wearing on me. But somehow I imagined that if I were smiling, my kids wouldn't know what was really going on. Raquel tried so hard to predict my needs and make me happy. She even taught Phillip how to walk! That was an amazing evening. We were all gathered around our family room and Raquel called Phillip and on cue, he let go of the table that was holding his wobbly little body and walked straight to her. We cheered so loud, Phillip did it for another 30 minutes walking to each of us as we called his name.

Smiling was not enough. They knew something was wrong. Obviously, I was the only bald Mom in school. If I had it to do over I would have been more open with them. But at 30-years-old, I tried to keep things as normal as possible. It wasn't until years later that Raquel voiced her insecurities to me. "How could I ever be as good as you. You had cancer and it didn't even bother you." Oh my, if I had only known she was feeling that, I would have been more vulnerable. I would have made sure she knew she never had to be like me, nor did I want her to. I wanted her and each of my children to be happy, just being them.

The more tired I became, the more difficult it was to stay positive. I focused my thoughts on my pre-operative procedures. I had to pick up my mammogram report and take to it to my appointment with Dr. Love.

12/28/1994
Oh God. I got my mammogram report today. Looks like there are masses and enlarged nodes on the right side as well as the left side. It looks like cancer. I am running around like crazy. Office to office. Picking up and dropping off reports. How do elderly people get this done? I am educated in the health industry. I know the ins and out's and I can barely keep my head above water and my own thoughts straight.

Suddenly I was in a state of the unknown again. There was nothing I could do until my appointment with Dr. Love. A thought keeps swirling in my head... "What if I do die?" Will I still end up losing both breasts? Too much too handle. So many questions and no answers. Breast, breast, breast. I don't want to hear that word ever again.

When we met with Dr. Love, I briefed her on the report and was in tears. Todd held my hand as I handed her my films and the mammogram report. She shoved the mammogram film into the backlit frame to look at it. She tilted her head back and slightly laughed. She looked at me and pointed to the film. "Look" she said, "These lymph nodes should be swollen, you've just finished nursing. And this area is where the cancer was removed." She continued to tell us that radiologists can't see pathology. They can only detect differences. This was serious. Dixie was so concerned, she knew of cases where a person becomes so distraught after a report that they committed suicide. Imagine a misdiagnosed report. My emotions were reeling. I just had to make it through another week and we would be completely on the road to recovery.

I was so afraid, I almost couldn't bear the thought of my future. My question "Why", had no answers. When I was alone, my mind would go to places that I could never discuss with anyone. I went to extremes many times. No one I knew had ever been through this. The only people I knew who had cancer had died. I trained myself to live in the present. I tried hard not to think about the negative possibilities. One day at a time. One day at a time.

December 31, 1994
My Mom had dropped off an envelope that said "Do not open until 1995". Hmmmm. It was 12:17am. I couldn't sleep. I had no idea what could be written in there. So I slowly opened the envelope. It was a guardian angel pin and a note that said how much she loves me and she would always be there for me.

Cancer is a funny thing. I knew my Mom, loved me, Moms HAVE to love you, right? I had resigned myself to the fact that she didn't really LIKE me.

01/02/95
Well it's midnight on the eve of my surgery. I haven't been afraid of the surgery until now. I am afraid of dying. I trust Dr. Love, but I'm still scared. If I die Phillip would never remember me or know how much joy he brought into our lives. Jordan would barely remember me. Raquel would remember me, but I'm sure it would grow faint. What would they remember about me? Would they remember the yelling and the rushing around? Would they remember how much I loved them? I am hoping the latter. All I have ever wanted was a family to love and care for. I do love them very much. Looking at them and watching them grow up is such a joy. I need to slow down and make sure they know how much joy they bring to me. This is silly. I just can't

shake this feeling. I know I'm not going to die. Okay I need to be more patient and reprioritize my life. Patience is what I will work on. They need to know I always love them. I am really worried about Raquel. I rely on her too much. She is so helpful and she helps me with everything. She helps me with delivering the magazines, she watches the boys. We are in for a rough year and I don't want her to slip into a role where she cannot be a little girl anymore.

If I could have one wish for my family it would be for my kids to love and cherish one another. To realize how special it is to have a family. I want a big, happy and loving family. That is my dream.

Surgery

My surgery went well. I didn't die. I was very sleepy and very sore. I woke up in the middle of it. I remember hearing people talking and I tried to move and talk but I couldn't. I just grunted. "Can you hear me?" A voice asked. That was all I heard until I was in recovery. Then the pain was strong. My left side was throbbing. I couldn't move my arm. As they sat me up the pain grew.

My nodes came back clear. Dr. Love said she got 23 of them and they were all clear! The resection of the tumor area was clear also.

I met with Dr. Chap, my oncologist and we talked about the different chemo possibilities. The team felt it was best to go with the "full guns" to make sure there wasn't a rogue cancer cell out there waiting to attach to something else and begin growing. I agreed. I didn't want to take any chances with this ever coming back. I would do the strongest chemo and radiation I could stand. They did tell me that after the chemo I would be infertile. The chemo would kill or damage all of my eggs. That was a painful revelation. I really had hoped for at least one more child. Now, there were no options. Don't get me wrong, I was grateful for the beautiful family I had. It just came as a shock.

I thought I would have a little more time before I started chemo, but I started the following week. I would definitely lose my hair in two to three weeks. I would be thrown into early menopause, and I have a small chance that the chemo would cause Leukemia. Dr. Chap said I couldn't take a sigh of relief for at least three years, and I couldn't take a breath of relief for 5 years. Forever I'll be afraid of it coming back. I was truly scared. There is no more life as I knew it. I jump to the thought of me being bald... Will people stare, or worse, laugh at me? Would I be ugly?

Will this affect my life span? Oh I had too many thoughts going through my head now. I was sure I wouldn't die, but every day I questioned it. I was really scared. I wish I had known someone to share all of this with. I didn't want to be a burden on my family, and I wanted them to know that I was confident. I didn't want them to know how afraid I was. I just wanted to live to be an old lady with my husband and watch my kids grow up. I wanted to be a grandma.

I signed up to be in a clinical trial. The drugs are the same strength or more. They are looking at the way it is given. One arm of the trial would be administering it in a different order. I wouldn't know which arm I would be in until the day I start chemo. Dr. Chap suggested I cut my hair short. She said it would be less traumatic when it began to fall out. I always give this advice to newly diagnosed patients that I meet.

In order to begin my chemo I had to have quite a few tests done for the clinical trial. They performed a new pap, a MUGA (Multi Gated Acquisition Scan... Radionuclide angiography) heart scan, a pregnancy test, urinalysis, and a few blood tests. During the MUGA they take some of my blood out and mix it with a radioactive material and re-inject it back into my system. Then they watch the chambers of my heart work. It wasn't bad at all.

As we were driving, I read the consent form out loud to Todd. Just reading about the chance of death and my cancer makes me cry. He's so supportive, but he's very scared too. I can only imagine how this is affecting the kids. I signed up for some counseling from the breast center for Todd and me.

I went in for my pap and apparently when my OB did it over a year ago it came back abnormal. I never knew that. I had to deliver my own pap to the hospital for quicker results. Now I have to wait. I still have to wonder how I can go through an entire pregnancy and the delivery and follow up appointments and not once did anyone mention an abnormal pap or feel my breast after I asked about the lump. My fears are getting the best of me. The "not knowing" is the worst. The waiting. I just wanted to cry and cry and cry. I wanted some time to think. I wanted to see my kids grow up and I was scared.

The lab called and my pap was negative. Yeah! All of that worrying for nothing. I had my hair cut off today. It actually looked cute short. It would take some time getting used to it. Oh, that's right I wouldn't have time to get used to it. I would be bald!

01/17/95
UCLA just called and my MUGA showed something abnormal. They want me to go in tomorrow and have an echocardiogram. Really? Can this really be? How messed up can one 29 year old be?

Starting Chemo

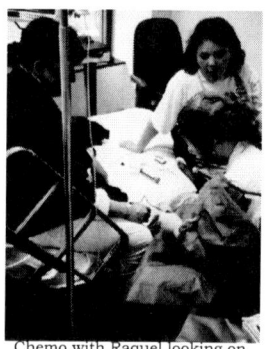

Chemo with Raquel looking on.

01/18/95
We went back to UCLA and they still found something a "little off, so they are having the cardiologist look at it. Either way I start chemo tomorrow. It may be a different kind, not as powerful and I may not be able to participate in the clinical trial. I met with the therapist. I talked about all of this and about all of the guilt I was carrying around. I didn't solve any problems, but it sure feels better. Todd will meet with her tomorrow during my chemo.

We arrived early for my chemo appointment. I made the clinical trial! I would be on the second arm of the clinical trial. The drugs will be given over the course of two days. I would have a dose on Thursday and come back for a second dose the following day. Wendy is my chemo nurse. I had a ton of questions for her. I didn't want to seem childish, but I had never experienced this before. She was more than nice answering my questions. "Will it burn when the chemo goes in?" "No, it won't" she said. "Will I get sick instantly and will I throw up?" "No" she smiled. "We are giving you a lot of anti-nausea medications right now and we'll send you home with a prescription for Compazine and Ativan. You probably won't get sick, you'll just be nauseated."

She started the IV in my wrist and started some fluids and medications. I started to get relaxed and a little sleepy. After a couple of hours she walked in with a full blue gown, a mask, goggles and heavy yellow gloves. She was carrying the Adriamycin, an orangey Jell-O looking tube of stuff. Like that description? Stuff- it's a clinical term.... Slowly she pushed the entire tube into my arm through the IV. She was right--no burning, no pain- nothing. I actually felt pretty good.

Todd had his talk with Carol. I'm so nosey.

I wonder what they talked about. I knew better out of respect than to ask and butt in. I didn't talk about what I said to her, I wasn't going to even bring it up.

We left UCLA and we were hungry. A few people suggested a little Italian restaurant, up the road in Westwood. But I was warned…don't eat any food that you really love right after chemo. Sometimes you develop an aversion to the foods you eat right after chemo. I felt so good, we went in and ordered a delicious salad and the most fabulous marinara over pasta. It had chunks of tomatoes and the bread was delicious. How could I ever not love that?

The next day I was scheduled for my second round of Adriamycin. We brought 11-year-old Raquel with us. She wanted to experience this too. I wanted her to know that it wasn't scary. I really think that if you are able to face things, then the unknown can't haunt you. We also had her stop by Carol's office for some "talking time". I never knew what they talked about. She was in there for a long time and she had been crying. It really breaks my heart to see her crying. I would do anything to make sure she never has to be faced with cancer. I tell her I'll be alright. I try and reassure her, but I'm sure she can sense that we are nervous. She's too smart and too aware of feelings to not recognize our fears.

The chemo made me really tired and nauseated. I have to start giving myself shots of Nuepagen, a medication that super-charges my bone marrow and keeps my blood counts high. Nuepagen increases the production of cells. I hope I can give myself the shots. It's daily for a week. I hate needles.

I wake up, take my shower, and get my syringe, alcohol pads, and the Nuepagen. I lock the door to the bedroom and I fill the syringe. I flick the syringe so there are no air bubbles. I wipe a little section of my belly, I squeeze it and I can't do it. It took me over an hour to give myself that first injection. I had myself crying so hard I could barely see, and honestly, I was getting tired of hearing myself. Finally I just held my breath and slipped the needle into my skin. I pushed the medication in and withdrew the needle. It didn't even hurt. All of that drama! Sometimes I make myself so angry. I am a drama queen.

My nausea is horrible. They called me in a new prescription for Zophran. $180 for 10 pills. My insurance won't cover it. I'll just suffer without it. My scalp is hurting, it's itchy. But I still have my hair. I can tell the shots are working. My bones ache like hell. It feels like I have a horrible flu and my body aches to the bone. My lower back and my hips are so sore. It's hard to walk.

It's a few days before my 30th birthday. While I feel like throwing myself a pity party. Raquel had planned a surprise party for me. We spent the day running around and in the midst of all the commotion, Raquel forgot about the party she had planned. Sweet little thing! She was so upset. Honestly just her making the attempt was the sweetest present I've ever gotten. She called all of my friends, and there were some presents on the porch when we got home. She called them and rescheduled it for next week.

I am trying to regain control of my mental status in regards to my cancer. Todd made a reference about me being sick. I told him to never refer to me as sick again. I'm not sick. I HAD cancer. Dr. Love said that as far as she was concerned it was in a jar in the hospital. My resection was clear, my nodes were clear. My chemo is preventative (adjuvant). It's precautionary. I HAD breast cancer. I am a survivor, not a victim. I am not sick. I'm not feeling well from the chemo. But I'm not sick. Todd did not deserve my harsh words. Man sometimes, I can be such a bitch. I hope he knows it's really me and not him. I appreciate him.

Losing my Hair

January 30th, 1995. I'm officially 30. I can't believe it. I still feel like I'm 20. We had a nice day and I still have my hair! I really thought it would be gone 7-10 days after my chemo. It's been over 2 weeks and I still have it. I thought maybe I would be the medical miracle and not lose it. My scalp does sting and itch a lot.

Two days later my hair started falling out. Every time I scratched my head a few strands fell out. Funny thing though, my head doesn't itch or sting anymore. That's actually a relief. It was really uncomfortable.

I decided that I would drive to my Mom's work. I pulled her into the stockroom at her work and said "Look." I tugged at the side of my head and a handful of hair came out. I started to cry and she just hugged me. I cried harder. I can't remember the last time she hugged me.

I drove home, and by then it was an obsession for me. I just couldn't stop plucking it out. I sat down at the kitchen table and slowly pulled. More and more it was piling on the table. I finally called Todd at work. He was in a meeting, and luckily, my friend Wendy answered the phone. She could tell I was upset and asked if she could do anything. I told her I had just pulled my hair out and I was freaking out. She offered to come over. Just talking to her was good. We talked until Todd came out of his meeting. He left work early, picked up the kids, and came home.

I was so embarrassed to show him. I looked horrible. I had sprigs of hair left and I actually looked sick. I wrapped my head in a towel and waited for him. He came in and I pulled the towel off. He looked at me and smiled. He cried and he held me while I cried. Finally we looked in the mirror together. I looked so darn goofy! We couldn't help but start to laugh. My face was so swollen and red and to top it off, my hair had fallen out in the shape of a reverse Mohawk! I had no hair down the middle of my head and hair on the sides. I looked like Grandpa Munster! We laughed until the kids came in. I'm sure they could feel the tension and to hear laughter must have been a relief.

Raquel said, "It doesn't look bad." Jordan looked and me and said "You look cute." Thank God for kids. Jordan told me that he was going to shave his head so he would be like me and we could be bald together. I told him one bald person in the house was enough for now! He was so cute. I did take Todd's electric razor and I shaved the Grandpa Munster hair-do. Now I looked healthy again--bald but healthy.

Early Advocacy

The past month has been horrible. All the uncertainty and questions. The unknown is the hardest. I think I've had every test imaginable. I've had two surgeries. I've had my first round of chemo. I've lost my hair. Now I have 5 rounds of chemo left. That's 10 more times of driving an hour and a half each way to UCLA and receiving the treatment. Now I'm getting into a routine. Chemo. Neupagin injections, and blood draws three times a week.

If I can stay well and not get sick, I think I might be able to do this. It's so hard to look into the mirror. When I look super close at my face, I just see my normal blue eyes looking at me. Normal….hmmmmm.

About 2 weeks after losing my hair, just I was getting used to all of these new aspects of my life. I got a call from the UCLA Breast Center. A very exciting call The Leeza Gibbons television show was looking for young women who were dealing with complete hair loss (alopecia) due to chemo or the disease alopecia areata. They wanted to meet me. I sent over pictures and did a phone interview. I was in. This was to be my first public appearance speaking about cancer and advocacy.

Todd and I drove down to Los Angeles, a few days before the taping, for a clothes fitting. Turns out, as a thank you, they were bringing in a stylist, giving us a new outfit, and a new wig styled by the infamous Jose Eber and his styling team. I was over-the-top excited.

At dawn, the day of the taping, our doorbell rang. "Yes, I'm here to drive Mrs. Post to the Leeza Show." It was surreal. Todd walked me out to the stretch limo. Riding down our little street to the freeway is a moment I will never forget. Four hours later the limo came back to pick up my family.

During those four hours the Leeza staff had 5 of us at the wig shop with Mr. Eber. He helped us pick out wigs. He would then do a custom cut and style specifically for each of us. I had watched Jose Eber's styling magic on television for as long as he was styling hair for famous people. I couldn't help but look at him and say, "Wow, the one time I get Jose Eber to cut and style my hair,…,I'm actually bald as an eagle!" The irony had all of us in stitches!!!

My dear childhood friend, Sharmane, came to the taping of the show. I could see

Todd and the kids in the audience. I was so nervous. We had to walk across the set without tripping, all the while hitting our marks AND smiling. It was exciting. Leeza Gibbons was amazing, and is still one of my favorite personalities. She was so real and so caring. Her true sense of being a people person shone through. This experience was well worth it. We each got to talk about how our illnesses were affecting us. We shared how family and friends were handling our hair loss. We even told stories about how strangers reacted.

As beautiful as the wig looked on me, it was so itchy and hot. I really didn't like wearing it. Even worse, I could see myself feeling pretty good and looking "normal," all the while my wig being half cocked. Phillip was now 9 months old, and grabbed everything. I couldn't expect him to keep his hands off of my hair. I decided to wear baseball caps. I had a nice black velvet baseball type cap that I was comfortable wearing.

February 14, 1995
Todd and I took off by ourselves and had dinner at Red Robin for Valentine's Day. I feel really yucky. I'm having a hard time eating. I ordered a chicken salad and I picked at it. I just don't feel like eating. I'm consumed by the thought of my kids. Even

the days when I feel okay, I get sick to my stomach when I think of them and what they are going through. On my worse days, I think about the worst possible scenario. Dying.

February 16, 1995
Today the kids are driving me crazy! Why won't they be nice to each other? They don't even try. We lost it tonight with them. Jordan got mad when he was asked to empty the garbage. He grabbed the bag and hit the car with it. Raquel put a booger in Jordan's mouth. They were doing real stupid and inconsiderate things. We sent them to bed early. I wish I had some help. I'm getting depressed. I don't know how to handle this.

Some days I feel like I'm losing my mind. I really don't want to do anymore chemo. What would happen if I stopped? I just feel like I'm on a roller coaster of my own emotions. Some days I feel fine. The next day I don't know how I will survive this.

My friends don't call to check on me and no one offers to take the kids. I know on the outside, I look like I'm handling all of this in stride, but I'm not. Can't anyone see how hard this is? I'm totally overwhelmed.

Chapter 3:
They Knock You When You're Down.

Rude Insensitive People

I'm still acting like all of this is normal. I use the appearance of normal to get through day to day. I just am at a loss of what I'm supposed to be feeling and how I'm supposed to be handling all of it. So I'm just ignoring it. But my brain won't shut off, no matter how much I tell myself "It'll be fine." I've started using the Nike saying "Just do it." It's become my hourly mantra. I write it on every piece of paper I can get my hands on.

I remember being in a store trying on clothes and I heard two ladies talking. "I wouldn't touch anything after she does. I am so afraid of getting cancer." Ouch! I just walked out, looked at them and smiled. What else could I do? Now I would have said a few things, but back then in 1995, I was in shock.

It wasn't only a regular group of people, it was the medical community, too. Phillip was running a high fever. We took him to the emergency room pretty late at night. I let them know that I was having chemo and I couldn't be near anyone who was contagious. They moved us to a room where there were no patients. We sat in there for a long time. Finally, an emergency room doctor walked in, took one look at me and said, "What's with the hat?"

Todd and I looked at each other in shock. I replied, "After you finish with my son, we can talk about me." Of course, he wouldn't let it go. I told him my story, and he replied with a few comments that left us dazed. "Well if you were my wife, I would have had you chop them both off". He continues. "I don't know what we're going to do with all of these people we are saving from cancer and all of these diseases, he reasoned, We are seriously overpopulating the planet and some people are just supposed to die off."

I know!!!!!! I couldn't believe it. Todd couldn't believe it. We left with Phillip. I was so angry I couldn't contain myself.

The next morning I called my friend, Carol, who was head of Public Relations at the hospital. I relayed every detail to her. This was a P.R. person's nightmare. It's not a good idea to totally offend a person who has access to airtime in a small community. It was even worse because I had produced newsletters for the hospital. I also produced a local cable television talk show "Community Healthcare Connection" with them.

I knew enough to let her handle it and she did. I will never forgot how poorly I was treated by that doctor.

Even today in 2012, I am amazed at how people react to me. I have done many radio shows on cancer. I have produced numerous TV shows from Los Angeles to Washington, DC, and have interviewed a lot of doctors, but many people are still ignorant to so many things.

Dealing with the thought of having cancer was bad enough for me. Then I had to endure the debilitating rounds of chemo. On top of all this, having to deal with the ignorant public and their reactions to me was almost more than I could bear. But life goes on. I still had a lot of work to do, and was publishing my local women's magazine every month. I was still doing the radio shows. I was still serving on my committees for the United Way and the Child Abuse Prevention center.

The only way I could juggle all this, was to have someone I trusted sell the advertising for my magazine. Unbeknownst to me, she saw an opening, and tried to capitalize on it for herself. The woman I had doing advertising sales for me had betrayed me.

I was in the middle of my chemo

treatments. I got a call from an advertising client who also happened to be a friend. She was crying and concerned about my health and asked me to please tell her what was really happening. I told her I was just finishing up my chemo and I was feeling crappy, but all in all, I was fine. She sighed a huge breath of relief. My saleswoman had called her, and apparently many of my clients, and told them that I wasn't doing well. They didn't expect me to make it, so she was going to take over my business. From now on, they should contact her directly.

I assured my friend that was not the case. There and then I knew I had to begin damage control. I fired my salesperson immediately. I was tired. I didn't feel good. People choose odd times to become selfish and greedy.

Each chemo was difficult. I felt worse with each one. My blood counts were dropping. I can't imagine how low they would have gone, if I didn't have the Nuepagin to bring them up. The Nuepagin brought my counts up quickly, but it was painful. The pain went so deep into my bones. It hurt to walk, it hurt to sit. It was like the flu times 100.

Towards the end of my chemo rounds, I talked to Dr. Chap. I literally felt like I couldn't take anymore Adriamycin. It was a struggle to move. She agreed to change the chemo to a Methotrexate. I did my last round of chemo with that.

After my chemo was done, I had a weird sense of needing to do more. But I quickly moved into the world of daily radiation therapy.

Radiation Therapy

Radiation therapy was different. I went in for consultations and measuring. The Radiation Oncologist wanted to target my treatments to the area where my surgery was done. The one thing that took me by surprise, was how they marked me for the radiation. I was tattooed in about 10 different locations across my chest, my breast, and my side. After all I had been through, you would have thought that these little pin pricks would have been a breeze. They hurt like crazy. The radiation technician would put the ink on a spot that had been marked out, and then put the needle in and kind of move it around to allow the ink to set in.

I have one that is small, well actually, it's tiny, right on my chest. When people are comparing tattoos I never hesitate to point mine out. I tell them it's God's view of the world.

The radiation procedure itself was a welcomed relief from the preliminaries. It was not invasive, or so I thought. I was alarmed at how exhausted I became. I went in for radiation every weekday for 7 weeks. My skin became red and painful. It blistered and peeled like a bad sunburn.

My hair began to sprout pretty quickly after the chemo stopped. It was light and short, but I could at least begin to feel it.

Pulling it all together

Todd, Phillip and me

After the radiation was finished, I felt a loss. My life had revolved around getting better. Now all I was expected to do was live a normal life. It was a relief to stop, but a panic set in.

As time passed, I became angry. I was mad at my friends who didn't call. I was mad at my body that betrayed me. I was mad that I was 30 years old and I had never experienced life. Todd was ready for a change too. He was from the East Coast and loved growing up in Connecticut.

I had heard so many great stories about his childhood and I just wanted to live a full life. I wanted my kids to have some fun. So he began to ask around to some of the company's affiliates about job opportunities.

It took only a couple of weeks. A television production manager, from the Jones Intercable affiliate in Alexandria, Virginia, expressed an interest in him coming there. The manager had worked with him over the phone. Todd had a great reputation for being knowledgeable, and a helpful problem solver to numerous affiliates across the U.S.

We had never been to Virginia, but both agreed to move there as soon as possible. I had barely finished my radiation and we were packing up everything. We were about to move to a place we had never even visited. Looking back, I think I must have been out of my mind. Talk about post-traumatic stress syndrome! I can't emphasize enough how important it would have been to talk to somebody and get some advice before making such a life-changing move. But I had just survived a bout with breast cancer. I wanted a good quality of life for my family, and we were already behind schedule.

Immediately after we moved and settled in to Virginia I was really happy. I felt great, and I loved my family. The problem was, I didn't have many friends, AND I HAD NO SUPPORT NETWORK. I spent all day by myself with Phillip. My brain was working trying to figure out what we had just been through. I sat on the bed and watched the OJ Simpson trial and the movie Babe over and over. I still couldn't grasp it. All I knew was I got scared. I just wanted to live. I have said this before, but it was a feeling that was getting more intense. I tried to start a little newspaper there, but my heart just wasn't in it.

I got involved with a local work from home moms group called Mothers Access To Careers at Home (MATCH), and I finally found friends. I began to blossom. I finally felt like I was getting back to "normal". I lost about 75 pounds from 227 pounds down to 150 pounds. I produced a children's exercise video called "Funky Fitness". I really was enjoying life.

I got a freelance job producing television for an educational network, called the Red Apple Network for Fairfax County Public Schools. thanks to my friend Sharon

Lawler. She worked part time there, and gave me a glowing recommendation.

I loved my job there. I was producing 5 different foreign language live shows. I was having so much fun! So I slowly began to pour myself into my work. My hours at work were weird, as all of my shows happened at night. I started working because I wanted my family to be proud of me; I wanted to accomplish something they could be proud of. I wish I knew then what I know now. My working wasn't going to make them proud, or impress them, or make them love me anymore.

At this point my kids were all in school; I was active in their life, all of the typical Mom things. When I went to work in the evening, Raquel would babysit until Todd got home shortly after I left. Life was good. The kids were being kids and driving us crazy.

Since it was a part time job, I took a temporary job with an international Arabic language network. It was all-consuming. ANA Television Network offered me a full time position. I talked to Todd about it and it had been my dream to produce television full-time. The kids were settled in and we created a new schedule for our family.

I created a new network of friends. I loved my job. It was exciting and different, and I was doing what I had only dreamt about. I worked long late hours in DC. I began to really feel like I was suffocating. Not by Todd, not by anyone except for me. I couldn't get it through my head that I was okay and I didn't have to fear living a short life. Nothing anyone could say, even the doctors, had me convinced. The best I could get from them was a resounding…"We don't know."

Wrong Turns

In 1998, I truly began to have a breakdown. It wasn't the kind of breakdown you hear about. It was a slow, methodical, painful breakdown. My mind just kept telling me to live! My life was very comfortable. But I wanted an amazing "WOW" life. I wanted to be treasured. Little did I know that I already had everything I was searching for, but I didn't figure all of that out until after I had grown away from Todd.

After many months of this, he finally asked me if I was going to leave him. And if that was what I wanted, to please do it now and not drag it out until we ended up hating each other. I didn't want to leave, I wanted both worlds. But he didn't ask me to stay. I just wanted him to ask me to stay. My self-esteem was at a very low point. I moved to an apartment, and we shuttled the kids back and forth. How ridiculous. I was such a fool. I ruined my life, Todd's life, and mostly, my children's childhood. I was selfish and I just didn't know any better. I was scared and childish.

I was lonely. I cried and I continued to search for someone to love me, okay really even just like me. I just wanted to be wanted.

I was let go from ANA Network. I was told it was due to financial difficulties. Honestly, I know I was let go because I was at work too much, and I was neglecting my family for work. My boss knew it, and he didn't like it. In hindsight, if I had only listened to that pip-squeak that called me out and let me go, I may have been able to salvage my life.

I was at rock bottom. My faith was wavering. I had stopped going to church, and my life had no guidance except for what I wanted to accomplish. Everything took a backseat to my needs and wants. It was a terrible time and I was in too deep to pull myself out. Once again, my pride stepped in and wouldn't let me repent.

I was determined to start a new life. One

with God at the helm. My life was in such conflict. I still knew God loved me, but I couldn't pull it together. I just needed some guidance, some friends with like minds and needs.

I began to get involved in a lot of motorcycle programming. I met a new man--Art Byrd. We fell into a very needy relationship. He knew that a relationship with God was at the top of my wants and needs. He happily took me to his parent's church. It quickly became my home church. It moved quickly and before I knew it he was living with me. He quit his job and I continued to work. This was the beginning of the downward spiral that led me to finally realize that I had made a huge mistake. Only now it was too late.

As if all if this weren't enough, after all of my previous chemo and all of the warnings of not being able to have any more children, I was pregnant. I was 35 and having a man's baby who wasn't my husband. Everything began to change between Art and me. We were no longer friends. He couldn't stand the sight of me. I couldn't stand being ignored. He wouldn't leave. He had no place to go. I continued to work and my belly continued to grow. My shame was unbearable. Luckily, I had the support of my childhood friend Sharmane and I was able to speak with her on a daily basis. It was clear that I was uncontrollably depressed. I wanted my family back, and that was no longer a possibility in my mind. Art suggested we terminate the pregnancy, but I couldn't do that.

I took an assignment, working as a producer for the state department, and scheduled to travel with a Bulgarian TV crew to shoot a few documentaries. The schedule kept getting pushed back. It was delayed until I was in my eighth month. My depression was beyond anything that I could control. How could I possibly raise a baby? I couldn't even properly take care of the three kids I had. I was still struggling with my feelings for Todd. The guilt was insurmountable. Financially, I couldn't raise all of my kids with out Todd's help. There was no way I could do this. I wasn't strong enough emotionally or mentally. I had strongly contemplated putting the baby up for adoption. I had a c-section scheduled for the week I returned to Virginia. All my plans were in order.

Somehow everything went out of my control...beyond any plans that I had made. After weeks of traveling with my crew, during the last day of shooting in San Diego, CA., I suddenly began to feel severe pains. My c-section wasn't scheduled for another two weeks. I had never gone into spontaneous labor before, but I knew something was wrong. My Aunt Tenie lived in the area and worked for an OB. I called her and she had me come in. I was already in labor! There was no way I could fly home to Virginia.

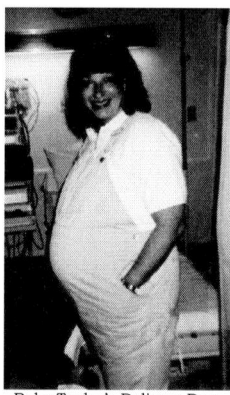

Baby Taylor's Delivery Day

I had spent the last several months planning how this event and subsequent life would unfold at home in Virginia. In one day, God had taken my life in a different direction. The next day the doctor took me in for a c-section and I delivered the baby in Chula Vista, California. I became her Mommy. She was astonishingly beautiful. She looked like Snow White. She seemed so tiny. I named her Taylor. Her father came in for the delivery and as soon as he laid his eyes on her he was smitten with her. Somehow it transferred to me and as her Mother he liked me too. Only it was too late for me, I had been shunned and ignored too many times.

As the days went by my depression was in full swing and I had no hope. Even with my new baby there was little to look forward to. I only saw myself as a failure. The thought that kept rolling through my head was "You've made your bed, now lie in it". "YOU SCREWED EVERYTHING UP!". I had heard it a hundred times growing up from my Mom.

At least Art was being cordial to me. We traveled home to Virginia and introduced Taylor to our friends and family. Art's daughter, Lauren, fell in love with her. We call Taylor, Lauren's mini-me. The similarities were amazing. To this day you wouldn't know they had different mothers. My kids met her and they too fell in love with her. Phillip became especially close to her. I buckled down into my new life and tried to do the best I could. I felt I would never feel true happiness again. I hated my life. I loved my kids, but I hated my life.

Art and I had been going to church regularly for months even before the pregnancy. It was my safe haven. Those were the only moments where I felt whole and complete. I wish I could have bottled that and sipped it whenever I needed a boost of comfort and love.

I knew that I wouldn't leave this relationship. I would live the life I had created. I would just make the best of it. December 31st of 2000 Art and I got married. It was a no fuss ceremony with only his parents, Taylor and Phillip attending. Todd sent Phillip in with flowers for me. My journal still has tearstains where I wrote this. I wore an outfit I had worn for a live event production a few years before. We went to a Washington Wizards game and that was that. We were a family, and damn it, I was going to make it work.

Chapter 4: ROUND 2!

No! Not Again!

In 2001, when Taylor was eight months old, I felt a lump in my right breast. I knew the feeling, it felt the same as last time. I had been going faithfully to my doctors. I made an appointment and my primary care doctor saw me right away. He confirmed that it was something that needed to be looked at and sent me to a surgeon. I couldn't believe it. How could this be happening again? Could my unhappiness, my self-hatred and loathing have caused this? I tried not to get into a panic until we had the results of the biopsy.

I checked into the outpatient section of the hospital and suddenly I was overcome by a fear like I had never had. Panic was setting in. I began to sweat, my head was spinning. I came out of the changing area to the holding area. Art was there waiting for me, he said nothing. I told him I was scared and he just looked at me. Nothing. I crawled into the easy chair and waited-- alone. They finally called me to go back and I laid down on the gurney waiting. Waiting and shaking until tears were down my face. No one was with me. No nurses, no family, no one.

A man in scrubs saw me and came over. He was the anesthesiologist. He held my arm and shared with me that he had just finished cancer treatment. He understood my fear. The empathy in his eyes was like a warm blanket. I felt a kindred soul with me and it made all of the difference in the world. He sat with me until I was okay to be left alone, promising that he would be right back with medication to ease the fear. He came right back and began sedating me. I fell asleep while his kind eyes watched over me. I never got the chance to thank him. I wonder if he is aware of how much he did for me.

All I can say is, you know your body. My biopsy came back malignant. A new cancer was present. This wasn't a recurrence it was a new primary. My life fell into more chaos.

Within a week, I had a lumpectomy and they did a sentinel node biopsy. This was a huge change and advancement from 1994. Instead of going in and scooping out a lot of lymph nodes they were able to single out the main lymph node that was responsible for the drainage of the tumor. It was a radiologic procedure where they injected dye into my tumor. We waited for hours until the sentinel node became obvious. I was then wheeled into surgery and only one node was removed as well as the tumor which had perfect margins. We were sure the tumor was safely removed.

At this point, my relationship with Raquel was very strained. She was angry with me and I didn't blame her. I was angry with me too. Raquel graduated from T.C. Williams High School in Alexandria, VA, that week. I was so proud of her. I was proud that I was able to watch this event in her life. When I was diagnosed the first time, I had asked God for this gift. I made it to the first graduation of my three children! Now I had a fourth graduation to pray about.

Moving Back Home

When I thought about my treatment options, I knew I had to go back to UCLA. I wanted to see my oncologist, Dr. Chap, who had treated me before. I had already had Adriamycin and was probably at my toxicity limit, so I thought I would be spared from the hair loss. I had another problem. I had to figure out how to get back to California. What would I do about insurance? Where we would live?

I called my family. My Mom and her husband helped. So did Art's parents. I was so excited to financially be able to get to California for my treatment. I started calling a few close friends back home and telling them I would be moving back.

One of the friends I called, Tim Rice, was a new friend we had met the year before at a motorcycle dealership convention. He owned a motorcycle dealership and was truly one of the nicest people I had ever known. He was a little kooky, but he was fun. I knew that we would be friends forever the day I met him. True to the meaning of friend, he said to come on out. Art could go to work for him, and when I felt better I could also work there. WOW!!! What an amazing offer. He also added an icing on the cake that was the availability of health insurance.

Needless to say, I was overwhelmed and couldn't turn it down. Maybe my luck was beginning to change. Things were falling into place. We loaded up and ironically moved to my Mom's house, the same house I was so eager to move away from when I was younger. If only temporarily, it would once again be my home.

My son, Jordan didn't want to leave his friends. Even though Raquel was living with me, she very angry with me and moved back with Todd and Jordan. Phillip wanted to come with me. He was still his mommy's boy. I know I needed him too. I needed to fight this and have hope. My kids were my hope. My rocks. My Angels.

I eagerly made an appointment when we arrived in California to meet with Dr. Chap. My medical records were shipped ahead. I was pretty confident that we had caught this one earlier than the last cancer. I had myself convinced that I wouldn't have to go through what I went through last time.

I met with Dr. Chap and we went over my results and she broke the news to me that I would, in fact, be using more Adriamycin. I would be losing my hair again! I cried. I cried all of the tears for all of the things I had been holding in. I cried because I didn't know if I could do this again. I knew what was in store, and I really didn't want to do it again.

Hell on Earth

My Mom's house had changed over the years. My former bedroom had been converted into the dog's and cat's room. My brother Shannon's room had long since been converted into a gigantic walk-in closet filled from top to bottom with my Mom's collection of clothes and goods that she couldn't bear to part with. We slept on the sofa bed in the enclosed patio that had been converted into a sporting room that housed the dead carcasses of their prize winning hunting kills. We had a stuffed taxidermied bear, mountain lion, some kind of bird amongst other things, as well as the kitty litter box. You entered the patio from the sliding glass door of the living room where the TV was always on. It's a good thing we didn't need any privacy!

Although not optimal, I was thankful to have a place to sleep. But if there was a hell on earth, I was in the depths of it. I was 35 years old living with my Mother, her husband, my husband who barely tolerated me, and my two children Taylor and Phillip. Not to mention the prospect of losing my hair within a few weeks. Oh, this was character building to say the least. God and I needed to talk. How much more character did I need? How much more suffering would I, could I, endure?

I was tested for many things again before my chemo was scheduled. It all happened quickly and before I knew it, I was in treatment again. I lost my hair. But I kept plugging along. I had no one to talk to. No one to share my fears with. I remember one night I was up alone and picked up a magazine. Rosie O'Donnell had written an article about the loss of one of her teachers. It struck me the wrong way and scared me. I cried. I tried to explain to Art what I was feeling. He just told me to not be stupid, and that I was being ridiculous.

I was still totally and completely alone and had no one to lean on.

Home for the Holidays

Mom, Grandma Grijalva, Raquel, Taylor, and me.

I needed to move to my own place. I needed to have my own domain where I could let my guard down. Where I could feel the feelings I was holding in. Art and I were selling little diecast motorcycle toys from our car when he wasn't working at the dealership. We finally made enough to rent an apartment where my stepsister, Christy, her husband and son lived. It was an upstairs unit and it was only $450 per month. We finagled our way into that place. I finally had a place where I could be nauseated alone. Totally and completely alone.

My marriage was a sham, a total joke. After my cancer diagnosis, Art was happy about getting to finally move to California. He was along for the ride. I knew this. He couldn't stand the most basic form of conversation with me. He would either say something cruel or just ignore me. I could walk into a room, address him, and get no response. It was eerie. No matter what I did, he would do the opposite. If I made dinner, he would not eat it. He would pick at leftovers or buy himself something to eat.

During my treatments, he was emotionally void of any sympathy. He ignored the obvious fact that his wife was bald and sick. If I expressed any fear or concern, he told me I was being stupid. As I finished my chemo and started my radiation, he completely abandoned me. Oh he still lived in the apartment physically, but emotionally he was gone.

I had to drive to UCLA for treatments. The gas money was eating us alive. I called the American Cancer Society to see if there was any help I could get. The local chapter had nothing. There weren't many places I knew to get any assistance. I especially didn't want to ask anyone else for help. There were no offers for help, and I just couldn't think of anyone who I could trust to ask without the fear of further humiliation.

I struggled to pay the bills. Not only financially, but trying to keep track of everything. Driving two hours each way for doctors' appointments and the endless supply of nausea battled for my attention, not to mention I was raising two children and carrying a tremendous burden of guilt for the family that I left in Virginia. On September 10, 2001 I came home to a dark house after my chemo. I hadn't paid the electric bill, and I was cut off.

My dear Sharmane

I called Sharmane in tears again. She had us come stay at her house until our electricity could be turned back on. I was thankful to be in a house with my friend and my children. Yes, Art was there too.

I woke up on September 11 in the "chemo fog" and to television reports that I thought was the news, but it was so horrific I was sure I must be hearing a movie--not the news. I sat in disbelief as I watched the Twin Towers crumble. It was like a scene from a Hollywood movie. Surreal. Devastating. And tragically real.

During the beginning of October, I finished my chemo and started the next phase of my treatment--daily radiation. This was two hours of driving myself each way to UCLA every day. Art was working at the dealership, so it was up to me to get back and forth. My step-sister Christy volunteered to go with me when she could, driving us and sitting with Taylor and her son Justin while I was radiated. Eating was difficult. I was nauseated, and after one of my chemo visits, Christy introduced the food of life for me, Jamba Juice. After the radiation, we would make our Jamba Juice run and rush back two hours to pick up Phillip and Justin from school. It was an exhausting couple of months, but shortly before Christmas, I was done. I looked forward to putting this phase of my life behind me.

My Dad was coming to visit for Christmas. He had never seen me bald, and we hadn't seen each other in many years. I was excited. As many problems as I had with my Dad, he was the person I knew loved me for me. His parenting while I was growing up was questionable, but he honestly always liked me as a person. This knowledge helped me quite often as an adult.

Two weeks prior to my Dad arriving, Art told me, very matter-of-factly, that he wanted out of the marriage. He was done. It was over.

I looked at him and asked, "Are you sure?"

He said yes.

I asked him the same exact question again the next day.

His answer was the same.

I began to feel a spark of life in me. He wanted out and I felt a sense of relief.

The day my Dad arrived I was so joyful and filled with a new sense of hope. I was doubly surprised when my brother hopped out of the car too! It was a total surprise! They had kept this a secret, and I hadn't suspected a thing.

Todd brought Jordan out to spend Christmas with Phillip. As happy as I was to see them and be with them, it was like opening a huge wound. I saw the husband that had been mine. My family was there. But so was Art. He had continued over the past few weeks to insist that this was his final decision. He wanted out. He didn't love me. He didn't like me; it was over. I was able to emotionally give up. I was free. My life was mine. It was time to reclaim it. I felt strong. My family was here and I was in my hometown.

Trying To Move On

Todd on his birthday after moving me into my new house.
Phillip, Jordan, and little old bald me.

I wanted a new start. I made a few calls and found a house that was available and I took it. While my dad, brother, and Todd were there, we loaded my few belongings up, and began to move them to my new house. Art could have the apartment. He was free. However, he did not take me up on the option. His free ride was over and he panicked. He packed his things and loaded them up and moved with me too!!! I should have known then and there that this was the day I should have put my foot down and said "NO, you stay here!" This happened to be Christmas Eve day.

Everyone was making a final load, and I was holding Taylor. Art drove off and left me stranded. I was walking to the car and he just left us standing in the driveway of the old empty apartment. I could see him looking back at me in the mirror. My dad and brother had just driven off. I was stuck.

All of a sudden, out of nowhere, Todd and Jordan pulled up. Todd asked me how I was getting to the new house. I just looked at him. I held Taylor close and hopped into his car. Filled with shame and embarrassment, I couldn't imagine how I got to this point in my life.

Todd took me to my new home. As I walked inside, I began seething with hatred. As always, I kept it inside. I didn't want anyone to know the humiliation I was experiencing. Nothing was ever the same between Art and I. I truly hated him at this point.

After everyone went home after the holidays I was left with my feelings, still pretty hairless and recovering from all of my treatments. It was time for me to pull myself together.

I began applying for jobs. Who would hire me? I was offered a job as a marketing director for a private park and event center. Slowly I came back to life. I was self sufficient again. Art still continued to hate me, but it was okay. The feeling was mutual.

Trouble with Art

One thing about me is that through all of these trials in life I have developed the patience of Job, but when I'm done, I'm done. Now I was done with Art, but I had to orchestrate my own freedom.

The situation was getting pretty bad. Art ignored Phillip just as he did me. It was not fair to subject Phillip to the type of treatment I had to endure. I would have been a negligent mom to have him go through this any longer. I had no choice but to call Todd and send Phillip to live back there. Once again my heart was breaking. I don't know that any pain I have ever felt, could compare to the pain I felt dropping Phillip off at the airport.

As I pulled each shred of dignity and pride back, I realized I had options. I just turned 36, and I was far from finished. I hadn't survived cancer twice to live my live a miserable depressed woman. I had lost everything except for Taylor.

Art had stopped going to work. I was once again the only one working. I made an agreement with Art that if he stayed home with Taylor, I would work and pay the bills. The only good thing I can say about him is he did love Taylor. I knew she would be loved and safe. I once again threw myself into work. I made a decision to work full time at the dealership. I stayed at my friend Sue's house, and drove to work from there. It was about an hour closer to work. I came home mid-week and weekends. Not the best decision in retrospect, but I followed the only path I knew. This went on for months. Emotionally I was doing better. Every day I was stronger. The break up with Art was easy for me to handle. I was relieved to be free from the commitment I had made. I was able to move on, and make plans for my future. I loved working at the dealership. I craved belonging, and Rice Honda provided me with a place to fit in. I was helping and growing.

I made friends, and I was feeling happy. Tim, our motorcycle friend, was a huge support for me. We worked well together and I was totally indebted to him for everything he had done. The things I found out after I started working there shocked me. Tim had paid out of pocket for my health insurance. Art made no attempt to repay him from his earnings while working at the dealership. My loyalty to Tim grew as did my respect for this generous, caring man.

I began to look for apartments near the dealership. I had no intention of taking Taylor away from Art, but I did want to have equal time with her. I found a daycare near work. It was time to move ahead and close this chapter of my life.

I let Art know that I had found a place and that I would be officially moving out. To my surprise, he freaked out. I had never seen this man show emotion, and now he was crying, begging me to reconsider. For me there was nothing to reconsider. It took me months to accept his decision, and to get my life together. He didn't want me. What he didn't want to lose was the financial support I was giving him. I had to call my Mom's husband, Art C., to come talk to him and I was in shock. Now it was I who had no feelings. My Mom and her husband had a special relationship with Art. I to this day have no idea what that emotional link was.

The next morning I got up and Taylor started her new school. I know he was heartbroken to see Taylor go, but I assured him that we would do our best to make our time with her equal and fair.

The Ultimate Betrayal

I took Taylor back to Art for the weekend. When I went back to get her, he had moved from the house. I was panicked. I had no idea where my baby was. I called my Mom. Very calmly they explained to me that Art and Taylor had moved in with them! They were going to protect her, and make sure I didn't take her and leave back to Virginia. I was in disbelief. They wouldn't make arrangements for me to get her, let alone see her. This I considered to be the ultimate betrayal. I have never found out the entire story. I have never asked. No answer would make me feel better about the situation.

I called for a week, begging each of them. I didn't want to traumatize Taylor by going up there and just yanking her from them. There was no way I was going to let this happen. Fortunately, my brain was back in motion and I was thinking clearly. I filed an emergency motion at the Orange County courthouse.

I explained the situation and was told by the judge that she was my child, and that I had every right to get her. I made sure that I wouldn't be considered a kidnapper, or get myself into any trouble. When I was sure that this was within my legal rights, I filed a new court date and did everything completely by the book.

Sharmane's niece was watching Taylor while Art was visiting dealers to sell the toy motorcycles. When I got the okay to get her, I drove the two hours from work and picked Taylor up. Sharmane instructed her niece to release her to me. I was so happy to put my arms around her! Yet my heart was beating so fast I felt like I was going to be physically sick. I buckled Taylor into her car seat and drove off.

I immediately called Art and told him that I had her and that we had a court date set for a few days later. He needed to show up. I felt a sense of pride. I was finally acting like a mother. I knew I was doing the right thing. I also knew I had no intention of taking her out of his life.

We both showed up at court and we went before the judge. We were sent to work with a mediator, to see if we could come up with a plan and avoid any further delays. It took us hours, but we did come to an agreement. He would pick her up Thursday from school, and I would pick her up Sunday afternoon. We were to split the cost of childcare 50/50. Nothing else.

This agreement lasted a week. He stopped picking her up after the first week. If it wasn't his way, he wasn't playing. Months went by before he took my phone call. He had left his older daughter, Lauren and it devastated her. Lauren's mom made every attempt she could to keep him involved in her life. He refused. His parents, however, were actively involved in Lauren's life. I saw how much Art loved Taylor. I had no idea he could turn his feelings off for her. But he did.

Months later, Thanksgiving of 2002, I made plans for him to meet us, let him see her and reacquaint himself. We set up a meeting at a restaurant. He never showed.

Tim and I had built a solid friendship, and it was growing. I couldn't believe this man who had known me while I was sick and bald, had seen me honestly at my worst, could see past all of that, and wanted to be with me. It was so easy and natural. I had a hard time with my beliefs. No matter how much fun we had, how simple things were, I couldn't let myself honestly believe that I "deserved" to be around a good man like him.

I also had a tough time because I was still dealing with my feelings for Todd. Did I really deserve to be happy? How could I possibly be happy and still feel so heartbroken about Todd? It seemed that the two feelings were irrational and just couldn't co-exist. Not a day went by that I didn't hate myself for what I had done to my family. It would take me ten years and Todd remarrying, to begin to feel a sense of release.

Many attempts were made on my part to reunite Art with Taylor. I set up two meetings which he actually kept, but he was detached and aloof. He borrowed money from me, and I paid for a motel for him to stay in. He made no attempt to keep in contact with me, and stopped returning my calls.

I wasn't going to force him into a relationship with Taylor. Lauren's mom, Becky, tried that with him and it didn't work. I feel so saddened because Lauren ended up being terribly hurt and experienced a loss that no child should have to feel.

Saved By The Bell

Our first Christmas together.

Soon Taylor and I moved in with Tim. We were so compatible, it was almost eerie. We did have our adjustment periods. He had raised his children. His youngest was graduating from high school, and now he was around a toddler and having to re-adjust. Being 12 years older than me, it was a huge adjustment on his part. Sometimes I didn't know if he would be able to do it. But somehow weeks turned into months, months turned into years and we married when Taylor was 4 years old.

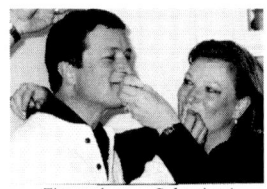

Our wedding with our Family by the beach.

Tim and me... Cake time!

Financially, the dealership was struggling. The war was taking a devastating toll on the economy. When we finally closed the motorcycle dealership, everything we had was gone. Tim took a job in North Carolina. We packed up and moved. Tim sold his house and we bought a new beautiful house on an acre of land in the North Carolina countryside. Tim started a new job for a non-profit that raised money for pediatric brain tumors. After being with him 24/7, it was quite an adjustment to have him working out of the house for more than 40 hours a week. I was lonely and didn't know a soul. The 40 hours a week I could handle, but the new job also entailed Tim to travel out of town for a few days a week as well. That was a surprise!

Our home in North Carolina.

We had been in North Carolina about two months when spring was beginning to erase the snow and grayness of the winter. Lauren, Taylor's older half sister by Art, was out for a visit and we were meeting Tim for lunch. Tim was taking his first motorcycle ride of the year. Closing the dealership had been devastating for him. His parents started it 40 years prior, and he couldn't help but feel that he had let down his employees and the entire Rice family. It was a joy seeing the spark in his eye when he pulled up on his bike.

After we ate, we had decided to go to a fundraising event, a horse show outside of town. I ran home with the kids to get my camera. Tim was stopping at the Auto Club to get some maps for the ride we were taking, just the two of us, later that afternoon.

The Accident

I pulled up to the house, jumped out of the car, grabbed the camera and the phone rang. We didn't know anyone, and I thought about ignoring it, but something told me to pick it up.

"Mrs. Rice?"
"Yes."
"I'm here with your husband Tim." the voice continued. "He's been in a motorcycle accident."
"How is he? Is he okay?"
"It's pretty bad, but he's awake."

The stranger gave me the location, and told me Tim was going to need to go to the hospital. I grabbed the kids, and traded from the car to our truck to be able to grab his motorcycle, then go to the hospital.

I drove up the highway to the spot where the accident was. The traffic was backed up. I could see the emergency lights ahead. Everything was moving in slow motion. I looked around, trying to find a way to get to him. As I looked around, I saw his motorcycle on the back of the tow truck, driving away. I hopped the curb, drove over some grass, until I got close enough to leap out of the truck and run to the scene.

There was a minivan and police all over. I tried as rationally as I could to ask where the rider was. How did it happen? Is he okay?

The police officer looked at me and asked who I was. I explained that I was his wife and a bystander had called me. My panic was rising. He then looked at me and in a slow southern drawl he said,

"Ma'am, your husband has been transported to the hospital by ambulance."
"Is he okay?"
"That's what they're going to find out. He was awake, though."
"How did this happen?"
"Ma'am," he said, "You see that minivan there? Well your husband plowed into the rear of it. He shot up underneath it and out from under the drivers side door."
"You mean it was his fault????" I said in total disbelief.
"Yes, Ma'am. We had to pry his motorcycle out from up underneath that minivan."
"Was anyone hurt?"
"Nope, just your husband."
"I'm going to kill him," I muttered.
"Now Ma'am that would totally defeat the purpose of getting him to the hospital," He said with a kind smile.
He directed me how to get to the hospital

which thankfully was a high-end trauma center.

When I walked into his trauma room, they had his legs tied together. You could see that his left leg wasn't right. The right one had shape, a knee, the left one was just a ball of swollen tissue. Only a little scrape, but it was unrecognizable as his leg.

The agony in his eyes was unbearable for me to watch. He had already had high doses of morphine, and he was in shock. They took him into surgery to determine what damage had been done. It turns out the swelling was so bad they had to attach an external fixator. This was a brace attached with screws to the outside of his leg through the bone of his thigh at the top and the bone of his ankle at the bottom. He couldn't walk. When he was released from the hospital, I had to put him in the back of our SUV, with the seats folded down, so he could be propped up in the back.

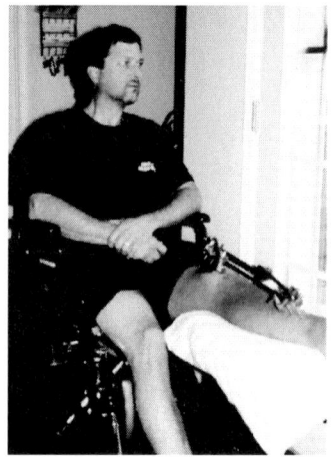

Tim and his external fixator.

We had to wait weeks until the swelling went down enough for them to go in and make any repairs they could. Each day was a regimen of cleaning the screws and the holes, so as to prevent any infection.

A week after the accident, the founders of the non-profit came over and "released" him from his job. We were told that cobra insurance would be made available to us at a cost of $1500 monthly. We were more than devastated. Tim had planned on doing his work from home. Calls could easily be made from there, until he was able to get back and forth to the office.

We learned a lot more about each other during the upcoming weeks. As with any serious illness or injury, we had to lean upon each other to get through the days.

He had been there for me. I was there for him. The orthopedist was amazing that did the surgery to repair the shattered leg. The hardware he has inside of his leg is like a piece of artwork. When we saw the x-ray at the doctors' office, we were acutely aware just how close he came to losing his leg. I truly believe if we were not at this trauma center, they would have had to amputate his mangled mess of a leg.

Chapter 5:
Majority Decision—GO WEST!

Moving back to California again

One of the blessings that we were able to recognize from this catastrophe, was that we really missed living in California. A majority of our kids were there. Our family and friends were there. As we sat in our living room day after day, we realized that we needed to move back home. It seemed that we would always find a reason to go back for a few days here, a few days there.

In August of 2004, we put the house up for sale, packed our things, and moved back to California. Of course, we had no home. We were renting a two bedroom apartment for Raquel so she could go to cosmetology school full time. We had no choice but to squeeze into there, until we figured out what we would do next. Happy days, Phillip moved back with us. I could have lived in a cardboard box. My priorities were getting straight. I had three of my four kids under the same roof. Tim's girls were nearby. This was beginning to look okay!

We ended up in Palm Springs. We rented a small house. We went to Mortgage Loan Officer School and worked on our real estate licenses. We both started to work for Tim's ex-wife's brother, John. Very quickly we both realized that this was not the career for us. However, John was great for us. Thanks John!! He was super supportive and accommodating. But Tim really missed what he knew best, and that was the motorcycle industry. He made a few calls and within a few days he was offered a job at a motorcycle dealership in Yucca Valley.

I went into the NBC affiliate, KMIR, a few times to see if they had any openings. I was called in to produce news promos for a temporary time. I loved the people, and I was having fun. It was strenuous. I would have to shoot the footage for the promo introductions, then take the footage that was being shot for the news, and create "compelling" reasons for people to tune into our news broadcasts. Too bad it was a temp job, it was really fun.

After that time ended, I quickly got a great job at Desert Homes Magazine selling real estate advertising. Life was coming together. I enjoyed being back in advertising sales. I was healthy. I quickly fell into the routine of doing all of my follow up appointments and enjoying my new life. There were just a couple of glitches. Like struggling with the company to get paid. After weeks and weeks of not getting paid, I had to quit. It was costing me money to do the job.

I met back up with the manager, Manny, from KMIR and lo and behold they needed someone for the afternoons doing promos and commercials. I'm nothing if not flexible. Hey, I had my family, I had hair, and a sweet husband. Life was good.

Tim and I had a weekly date night. Thursday nights in Palm Springs were the street fair. Sometimes the kids came with us, but tonight was going to be just the two of us. He drove the truck to the shop for some repairs and threw his motorcycle in the back for the ride home.

Here we go again!

The desert had been barraged with storms and rain that winter. Since the desert isn't typically caught up in rainstorms, the street drainage isn't set up to dispose of huge amounts of water quickly. We had a few roads wash away, and they were getting ready to reopen the next day. For months, Tim had been riding his street bike back and forth to work, taking the long way around, until the road was reopened. He called me as he was leaving work to tell me to get ready. He was off work and heading home on his dual-sport motorcycle. If the road still had a bad spot, he could take a quick detour off road no problem.

He worked about 45 minutes from home so I had plenty of time to get dressed and make the kids something for dinner. After I had cleaned up, I looked at the clock and decided to call Tim. Occasionally he would get caught up with a customer as he was walking out, and he would lose track of time. No answer. I got this uneasy feeling. I took the trash out to the cans in the back. I heard sirens. The fire department was only a few streets up. We always heard sirens so this wasn't unusual. But somehow this time the sirens scared me.

I ran into the house and looked at Raquel, "I need to eat," I said. "But you're going out." She looked at me as if I was crazy. I looked at her and told her I had a weird feeling that something was wrong, and I wouldn't have a chance to eat later. She laughed and said I was being paranoid. I did have a tendency after Tim's accident to worry about him unnecessarily. That's why he got into the habit of calling me before he left work.

The minutes ticked by. Each minute seemed to take an eternity. About 45 minutes later the phone rang. Raquel and I looked at each other as I picked up the phone.
"Mrs. Rice? This is the nurse from Desert

Regional Hospital. I need for you to come down here. Your husband has been in an accident and he is unconscious."

I grabbed the keys and unknowingly skidded out of the driveway and up the street. Thankfully the hospital was only about 5 minutes away. I pulled up to the emergency entrance and ran inside. The ER was packed. There were people all over the place. Every room was filled. I couldn't find Tim. They finally led me down the hall to a makeshift room where I saw his legs poking out from behind the screen. I tentatively rounded the corner and there he was, laying on the gurney. "Tim?" "Tim?" The nurse said he had woken up but was still out of it. I asked if he reinjured his leg. He opened his eyes and peeked out a small smile. Relief washed over me.
"What happened???"

Just as he was waking up the police entered the area. They overheard me ask about his leg. I told them nine months earlier he had been in a pretty bad accident. I asked again what had happened. They explained to me that he was found on the side of the road in a ditch. They only reason they even found him, was another passerby saw the light from his motorcycle headlamp. I didn't understand what they were telling me. He drives the freeway home, but no, not tonight. He wanted to get home early. We had date night, just the two of us. It was our honored special time.

He was driving on the road that was still closed and was scheduled to open tomorrow. He was almost home and he ran into the road block. The police were not happy. He went around the barricade, they explained. The roadblock consisted of an elongated triangular steel tube attached to the other side of a pole with chain link and a lock.

"Were the signs down?" I asked.

No. He disregarded the signs and went around them. Oh no, this was not possible. This was the man who never disobeyed the law. Tim was the ultimate "Boy Scout." There had to be some mistake. Oh, there was no mistake, and they were there to place him under arrest. As I pleaded his case for him, assuring them that he would never do anything like that, he chimes in, "I just wanted to get home to you sooner Honey." Oh how I do love this man, but NOW??? He chooses now to become lucid and give his piece of the story. The officers looked at me, I looked at them. I quickly began to explain what had happened the past year, the closing of the dealership, the moving across country, the accident, moving back and, now how he worked for the dealership in Yucca Valley.

"Oh, he works at Hutchins?" one of the officers replied.

"Yes! He was on his way home to meet me for a date night at the street fair." As I see their faces begin to show some sympathy, one of the ambulance workers comes out and says, "Dude, we just saw you on the news. Channel 4 just did a report about your motorcycle accident." Oh great, now my work was involved… I smiled sheepishly at the officer. I guess they figured my hands were full enough. "Okay this time we'll give him a ticket, but we really should be arresting him."

"Thank you, thank you." I kept saying.

I hadn't had time to pay attention to what the doctors were doing with Tim. His arms were both curled up and he couldn't move them. I looked down at his helmet and saw blood on the inside, dried against the face shield. I felt a wave of nausea hit me like a ton of bricks. Suddenly, I looked at him and saw how serious this was. Then I got mad. It became about me. How could he have been so irresponsible, and put me in this position again!!!!

Everyone was saying that he was lucky to be alive. He was still gripping the handle bars upside down on the bike. The only way he was found is because the other driver was illegally driving there also. If the other driver hadn't shown up, I would have looked for him in the wrong place. I never would have thought of looking for him there. I never would have found him. Once again, our God was watching us. Although my faith has been very tested, it is very strong and supports me in the darkest, scariest of times. Now was one of them.

I left the room, walked out front to move my car from the emergency parking, and I called his sister, Carol, and her husband, Bill. I explained to them everything and then I lost it. I was crying. I was scared, and I was hopping mad.

True Love Injury

Tim was released, and needed to go back to the orthopedic surgeon the next day. As we met with the doctor, he looked at us and said. "Well this is a true love injury." What was he talking about? "You'll understand" he said and dropped it.

When we scheduled Tim for surgery, both of his arms were in as bad of shape as his leg was nine months earlier. They were swollen beyond belief. And they needed to be reconstructed. We were still paying for our COBRA insurance from the non-profit but somehow there was a problem with the insurance. We couldn't get the surgery scheduled until they had $5,000 cash. This was after they made us wait two weeks to find out about the insurance problem.

Oh and about the true love injury... we have to laugh now. We get it. Tim could do nothing for himself. He couldn't feed himself, couldn't go to the bathroom alone, couldn't shave, brush his teeth, dress, but the one that has had us in stitches was showering. The first time I had to shower him was quite an experience. I had helped him before when his leg was broken, but he controlled the soap action. Now, I was in control of washing the unmentionables.

I lathered up and washed his hair. That was easy. I headed south. As I started, the "Oh man, you have to be careful!" started. Hmmmm, this wasn't going to be as easy as I thought. I tried it several times and could tell it was uncomfortable. All of a sudden I had an idea. "Turn around", I told him. I had to treat his parts, as if they were my own. Carefully I placed my arms around his waist from behind. I soaped up and gently began to wash. I can still picture how this must have looked. We got so tickled that this memory actually became a fond highpoint of this time. Needless to say, I got pretty good at handling the equipment!!! And thanks to the person who invented the shower hose!!!! Yes, the true love injury part was sooo true and I still love him to death.

Coming up with $5,000 cash was impossible. We had lived off our savings and were able to sell our house in North Carolina, but we broke even on the sale. As a last resort, we asked Tim's sister, Carol, and she came to our rescue. Thanks Carol!

We finally got the insurance straightened out, and he had his surgeries. On the first round, they had to do the external fixator on one arm. The other was re-broken and repositioned.

We began to feel as if we were victims of a cruel plan. How could things get any worse? Never ask that!!! At least we always kept our senses of humor. It could be worse. I had survived two cancers. He had survived two accidents. We were happily married and we had each other. But we often looked at each other and wondered what was in store for us.

He continued to work for Hutchins.

definitely not the best poster child for selling motorcycles--a limping, two broken-armed salesperson. But they kept him on, and he continued to sell.

The hour-long drive was wearing on him and the summer was quickly upon us. I hated the miserable high heat in the triple digits. The only saving grace was that the house we were renting had a pool. Then the filter pump went out, and the property manager was in no hurry to fix it. The sparkling blue pool turned into a disgusting hazy green. The final straw for me was when the air conditioner went out. I can put up with a lot, but when it comes to being overheated and sweaty, I am down-right unreasonable. Try living in triple digit heat with no air conditioning, and a green pool!

I finally called the property manager and threw a full blown fit. Just like a spoiled brat. They agreed to put us up in a hotel with air conditioning, and they let us out of the remainder of our lease. That was my long nine months in the desert.

New Chapters. New Beginnings?

We ended up in a beautiful little farming town named Camarillo in Ventura County, CA. No sooner than we signed the lease on the house in Camarillo, Tim found a job to help with a new dealership opening in the Palm Springs area. It gave him some sanity and we needed the money. But it meant Tim would have to stay in the desert during the week, and only come home on the weekends.

Phillip, Taylor, Raquel and I started our lives in Camarillo.

For some reason, during this time I developed pneumonia. We had no insurance. I kept going to the urgent care paying cash and getting breathing treatments. I figured it was allergy based, since we were in the middle of a huge farming area, and there was really nothing I could do. I felt like crap most of the time, and couldn't get rid of the congestion. I was becoming more depressed and fatigued. Who needed this?

Blessing in Disguise

This time of my life was a blessed time for me. More like another blessing in disguise. I missed Tim terribly and felt horrible. I threw myself into reading books at night. My best friend, Linda Koss, recommended "The Secret of the Shadow" by Debbie Ford. This was one of the most difficult books I have ever delved into. It made me face my own hostilities and anger. Even though I thought I was past most of this, there were still lingering issues that I worked through. I came out of reading this book a more aware person.

Linda Koss and me.

I learned that I wasn't as angry with my Dad for leaving as I thought I was. It wasn't his fault, how my Mom treated me after he and Shannon left. It was my Mom's. She made her choices. He made his choices. He reconciled with me many years prior, yet I just couldn't let it go. This book helped me to understand the power of choice, and of letting go. He had made his apologies and I understood them fully now.

God has interrupted my life on many occasions. This was another one of those times. In December 2006, as I finished the book and feeling a sense of comfort, I got a call from my Dad. His hip was in terrible need of replacement. He lived in Hawaii and the wait time for this procedure was 6 months to a year. He had already been on narcotic painkillers for months. Both he and Shannon didn't know how much longer he could go on in this much pain, taking this much medication. Tim and I offered him to come and stay with us where we could work on getting him seen sooner. I honestly felt like I had won the lottery. And I let him know how excited I was. I had not lived with this man in over 25 years. He and I had a good long distance relationship. We spoke often on the phone and kept in touch with each other on a regular basis.

My Dad flew in from Hawaii and I anxiously met him at Los Angeles airport. He hobbled like a little old man and I barely recognized him. He was in so much pain. Sweat was dripping from his face and he moved slowly while he pushed a wheelchair with his belongings in it. The next month we worked hard at getting him into the orthopedic surgeons office. Once we were in, it was only a matter of months before he had his first hip replaced. He was a new man. He definitely was a pleasure to have around the house. He cooked some of my favorite childhood foods, and I heard more stories about his crazy life than I knew he had to tell. Six moths later he had the second hip replaced. What an amazing surgery.

Tim outside of his "Timobile".

Tim was still living in Palm Springs in his motorhome, Monday through Friday; working at the new dealership. We missed having our family together. So often we contemplated Tim just coming home and making everything work here. We would do what we needed to do. There was a dealership nearby in Ventura and Tim knew the manager. This was a hard time for Tim because in his mind, motorcycle dealer management was all he knew. He had stopped by the local dealership numerous times just to say hi. They always asked if he would come to work there. Finally Tim said yes.

Tim drove home and our family was together again. We started making plans for him to open his own ATV and Dirt bike training school. He signed up for the training and threw himself into getting the instructors license and we started the search for a place to open up a school.

I started a new women's magazine "South Bay Woman" with Linda and looked for part time work. I found an ad on Craigslist for a motorcycle adventure school that needed a bookkeeper. I called and made an instant connection with the man on the other end of the phone, Jim Hyde. I ended up talking about Tim and we made arrangements for Jim, Tim and I to meet. He was a couple of hours from us just outside of Castaic, CA. I got the job reorganizing his books and Tim worked with him doing Adventure Camps for dual sport motorcycle rides. We were spiraling down financially. It was getting worse for us.

Moving Closer to Mom

My mom was getting more forgetful. I was worried about her. I didn't know what to do. For me, being in control was the only way I knew to make things work. I had survived two cancers and I wanted to help my Mom. Only my help wasn't wanted. It didn't matter. I needed to help her. I needed to make all of the things right that had gone wrong with her during my life.

Sharmane moved to Georgia and so we decided that we would move into her house. So Tim, Phillip, Taylor, my dad and I all moved to Palmdale to be closer to my mom. Tim drove to Jim's Rawhyde Adventures Ranch for work. Our rent was cheaper and I was 15 minutes from my Mom. Even though we moved, I was still not feeling good. My congestion was better, but I was so tired. I started getting dizzy. As soon as the feeling would start, the only thing I could do was physically jump up and try to make myself breathe. I had to catch myself on many occasions to keep from falling. Still, things were moving in the right direction.

Our life was pulling together slowly. Tim applied for a corporate job with Kawasaki Motors. It was a few months-long process. In the meantime, he continued to work at the ranch. I think he was making $15 an hour. Jim, the ranch owner, was incredibly nice and saved our butts during this time.

After a long couple of months of following up with Kawasaki Motors Corporate, he was finally offered a job. It was about two and a half hours away in good traffic. So once again, he loaded up the motor home, parked it in our friends Dennis and Julia's driveway in Anaheim, and went to work in Irvine. Thank you Dennis and Julia!

The kids and I stayed in Palmdale and Tim drove home on Fridays. We were looking for a place to live closer to his work. Sharmane had the house we rented on the market, and we helped show it for her while she was in Georgia.

Life was beginning to feel normal. Tim had a job he could settle into. He liked the people, and felt welcome at his new job. During this time as I watched him make this transition, I learned more about grace and humility than I had ever before witnessed. He did not let his ego guide him, he let his love for our family make the decisions that led him to take this job. God was in control, and my husband was and continues to be a worthy servant who did what was in the best interest of our family.

At 42 years old, I was still very impulsive and eager to settle down into our "perfect" life. I found a very small, overpriced house 20 miles and up to a 45 minute commute from Tim's work in Huntington Beach. We missed the beach, and this house was within bicycle riding distance. We met with the landlords and they liked us. I thanked God for our good fortune. Silly girl, when will I learn the lesson that when I force something to work the way I want it to, it does not mean it is the right thing. This is what I wanted, what I prayed for. We sold the motor home for our deposit on the rental house. First and last months rent and the deposit. That was a lot of money. Money I didn't respect or appreciate at the time. My own ego was in charge and I wanted everything now.

In my mind we had paid our dues--over and over--cancers, divorces, closing a business, moving across the country, accidents and on and on. I didn't listen to my husband and his concerns, I didn't listen to what God was telling me. I was listening to my own wants and needs. The magazine was growing and we were finally making some money. Then I found a perfect job the week we moved into the house. I was hired to work as a producer on a new international television show in Newport Beach, CA called "Your Cancer Today." I was thrilled.

If you were to look at exactly how my life would look if it were perfect, this would be a snapshot. Beach living, my kids were settling in, Tim's dirt bike school was starting out, he was happy at Kawasaki, and I had an ocean view office. I was making a difference in lives. We were pulling together information, live saving information. Every week when we went to the studio to tape the show, I beamed with pride. Pride knowing that we were producing not only a television show, but, life saving information filled with hope. We were producing hope for people with questions and fears.

From the moment we moved into the Huntington Beach house it seemed problems abound. Promises made by the landlords to repair and fix things were never done. Tim did them himself. Then the roof needed replacing. The landlords hired a crew to do the replacement which turned out to be a huge mess with nails left in our front yard where the kids played, and a majority of our items we had stored in the garage were ruined because they had to take the roof down to the beams and studs.

Trying to Move Forward with Zero Energy

I enjoyed my work and it was very

demanding. The owner was definitely someone who had no trouble saying what was at the top of his mind--regardless of how it made others feel. I didn't then, and never have operated like that. I spared people's feelings at every opportunity. I tried to lead my life by example. I tried to treat others the way I wanted to be treated.

I was getting tired. Physically I just couldn't keep up. After a day at the office, all I could do was come home and go straight to bed. I couldn't stay awake. Soon, every minute I had at home was spent in my room sleeping. I knew something was wrong. My first thought was my cancer was back and it had metastasized to my brain. But I told no one. On top of this, I still had my commitment to our magazine, "South Bay Woman".

I was doing such a good job at work that the owner moved me from the production side of business to being his personal assistant. The exhaustion was stressful and it was too much for me to handle. I went to a series of doctors' appointments and ended up at a cardiologist's office having an echocardiogram.

The diagnosis was made quickly and positively. I was diagnosed with congestive heart failure and cardiomyopathy from the over toxicity of the chemotherapy agent, Adriamycin. My pumping function was a very low 27-29%. We were given all of our options, pros and cons, and a tentative plan. None of which would work for sure. There were drugs that had been used to rebuild heart failure from natural causes, but not too much research on hearts damaged by chemo. We decided to start those immediately, and take our chances. We did not know how my heart would respond. Our next option was to talk about a heart transplant. Tim looked at me and made the monkey joke we had used a few years before when his arms were removed from the casts. When he had to scratch his head, he looked like a monkey! He quickly looked at me and said with a monkey sounding "ooh, ooh, yee, yee I'll always love your monkey heart."

It was during this diagnosis that my friend Linda decided to have her daughter "help" me with the magazine. I gave her all of my passwords. Before I knew it, I was locked out of the magazine. No returned phone calls and a 25 year friendship sacrificed to have 100% control of this business. I was too tired and angry to fight over it. I was so hurt by her actions and I lost my best friend.

My Angel Doctor

Lisa Curcio, MD and me.

The doctor put me on disability and started medications to see if we could stabilize my pumping function and keep it from dropping. During this time I reflected on a very powerful interview we had done for "Your Cancer Today". I had invited a local breast surgeon, Dr. Lisa Curcio, to the show and speak to us about the new advances in breast cancer. I shared with her my excitement of having her as a guest on the show. I also shared that I was a two-time breast cancer survivor, and still filled with so many unanswered questions. I was excited to hear everything she had to say.

She quickly stopped me. "Have you ever been tested?????" "Tested for what?" I asked almost sarcastically. I thought I had been tested for everything under the sun. This happens to be the most pivotal point in my story. "Have you ever been tested for the BRCA gene?" Oh no, I explained. They told me I had no family history. Once again she stopped me, looked me straight in the eyes, and told me that just by virtue of me having had two breast cancers before the age of 50, I needed to be tested. Her next question was, "Tell me, has anyone at all in your family ever had any kind of cancer, ever."

My paternal grandmother was the only person in my entire family that had any kind of cancer. The next question, "How old was she?" I didn't know. She was my grandma so she seemed old to me. She was sick most of my life. She really struggled with a double mastectomy and surgeries. I did some quick math and figured she died in her early fifties.

She stressed the fact that this was a test I HAD to have. It wasn't an option. She couldn't believe that the BRCA test had never been offered, let alone encouraged. I took her seriously.

During this time of dealing with my heart, I made an appointment to see Dr. Curcio as a patient. She sat me down and went over all of the information regarding the details and implications of being BRCA positive or negative, and how either would help to manage my care. After all, two breast cancers before 35 years old is not common.

As she showed me statistics and numbers, I knew why she was so insistent. I suddenly saw myself reflected in those numbers. I wasn't alone. My blood was drawn, and papers were signed. My test was shipped off to a lab in Salt Lake City, Utah. Myriad Genetics would be the one examining my blood.

"DeAnna, Your Test Results are In"

Two weeks later I was called back in for my results. Dr. Curcio looked at me and told me I was definitely BRCA1 positive. I finally had answers. My cancers were not from something I did wrong, nor was I being punished at all. This was science. Genetics. Which I came to learn, all cancers are.

I swear the angels were singing and my grandma was smiling down at me.

Then the reality of what this diagnosis implicated, started to be further discussed. Prophylactic (preventative) removal of my fallopian tubes and ovaries was recommended. Prophylactic double mastectomies and reconstruction, if I opted for that, was also recommended. I was in!!!! I would do anything I needed to do, to make sure I never had to be diagnosed with cancer again.

I was referred to have CT scans of my abdomen and more blood tests. Everything came back normal. I went to the gynecologist where they did a trans-vaginal ultrasound that also came back clear. In light of all of the good news, the gynecologist I went to for a consultation felt I was too young to have my ovaries removed. She just wanted to watch my ovaries and would not do the surgery.

I reported this back to Dr. Curcio and she couldn't believe it. She was on the phone with her personal gynecologist, Dr. Kathryn Cvar, and scheduled an appointment for me immediately. Dr. Cvar looked at all of the information and knew that I needed the surgery in order to prevent more cancers. I opted for a full hysterectomy. It didn't make sense to me to go in and remove only part of what could safely be removed. Frankly, if I didn't need it, and it had potential to harbor these cancer cells...it had to go!

Just Preventative Surgery

I had a laparoscopic hysterectomy. It was an easy procedure for me and I felt great. Recovery was especially easy compared to three c-sections. Dr. Cvar was leaving on a quick vacation and she said everything looked good. No reason to worry.

A few days, later my phone rang and Dr. Curcio was on the line. "DeAnna your pathology came back and you have cancer". I was in disbelief. "Where?" Was all I could say. "They found cancer in your ovary. They are saying its metastatic breast to your ovary". "Hang on DeAnna…." I could hear her speaking to someone else, "She is BRCA positive. You need to go in and recheck the tubes. They need to be serial sectioned. Check them again!"

"Okay, DeAnna, I'm back. They are going to do some rechecking and I'll get back to you as soon as possible. Are you okay?" I couldn't breathe. All I could do was sit there. "I'll be fine", and we hung up. I cried. This was totally unexpected. Everything was fine. This was supposed to be a preventative surgery. This was a token surgery. Everything was supposed to be fine.

I was just getting my life back. I had just taken a job as an account executive for "Today's Woman Magazine" in Orange County. My heart was getting better. God, what is happening? What am I not learning? What do you want from me?

What do I need to do? Please God, hold me, and tell me what I need to do.

Welcome to the world of HBOC- Hereditary Breast and Ovarian Cancer.

I gathered myself and called Tim. I don't remember too much after that. Metastatic breast cancer. Ovarian cancer, I knew enough about both and neither option was good.

It was during this time that Tim's brother Mike, my dear brother-in-law, became critically ill and passed away very quickly. Mike and I had just enough time to joke about us Rices having a recovery home where we could get better together, and then he was gone.

I was dealing with his sudden death and the prospect of my own. Watching my sister-in-law, Sharon and the entire Rice family handle this tragic time with grace, confidence, and acceptance, was a life-changing experience. They taught me so much about humility, and how having a strong faith in love that God offers to all of his children is the ONLY way we can ever be all right after such loss. It translated to every area of my life. Nothing seemed fair. But as a family, they reminded me to fully trust in God's power and love.

It was time for me to figure out what was next in my journey. I was thrust into the new world of gynecological cancer. I had several referrals to gynecologic-oncologists, who specialize in cancers of the woman's reproductive system, and began to try to connect with the one who offered the most hope for my future. The one I chose, Dr. Jeb Brown, received the pathology report that diagnosed this cancer as metastatic breast to the ovary. He immediately referred me to a medical oncologist, a doctor who treats cancers in general. The difference between the diagnosis and resulting treatments could have been the difference between life and death for me. We had the lab send over the final pathology report that confirmed it was indeed a new fallopian tube cancer that had metastasized to my ovary and abdominal washings.

Panic time was setting in. We had sent the biopsy samples off to three different labs for confirmation and they all agreed it was a new primary fallopian tube cancer!!! I sent the results from all three labs to Dr. Brown's office and could only wait rather impatiently. During the short wait, I did meet with another gynecologic-oncologist at UC Irvine. Right from the start of the meeting, I knew she would <u>not</u> be the one I was going to be collaborating with to save my life.

She was snide. She had inside jokes with her associate. After sharing my history with her, she stopped, looked at my husband and charmingly said, "And you married her, even after you knew about all of her problems?" Somehow that was supposed to lighten the mood. Neither of us found the humor. What an ass!

She went on to discuss when she could fit me in, to do the de-bulking surgery. She had a vacation for two weeks, and then she had patients scheduled, so in about a month I could schedule my surgery. "A month?" I questioned. She turned and looked at me and said "Listen, your cancer is no more important than anyone else's." I looked at her, I agreed, and we walked out for good.

Chapter 6: Round 3

Not So Routine Surgery

Dr. Brown would be my surgeon come hell or high water. He got all three copies of the labs and they immediately made me an appointment to come in for a consultation. From the second Tim and I shook his hand and looked into his eyes, we knew we could trust him, and he was going to be the one to get us through this next chapter.

We scheduled surgery to do the de-bulking and discussed the chemotherapies we would be using. I would, for the third time, lose my hair. This would be a tough battle and it scared me. As I've said before, it feels so comforting to be on the knowing and the fighting, if you will, side of this.

The de-bulking was more than I expected. I had major complications during the surgery. A large, critical vein to the heart, my vena cava, ripped open and caused a lot of blood loss. They had to search for the tear, repair it, and then complete the rest of the surgery. Instead of the scheduled 6-hour surgery it turned into a 10-hour marathon. I lost over 800cc of blood during the procedure. When I woke up in the recovery room, there was to a scurry of people buzzing around me. "Are you with us, Mrs. Rice?" voices kept asking.

Fortunately for Tim, his sister Carol and her husband Bill, who married us, came up from San Diego to support us. They waited with Tim in the waiting room. We thought the surgery would be a few hours; it turned out to last all day, and they stayed the entire time.

Initially, it felt like a normal wake-up from recovery. Except everyone was scurrying around. They had machines coming in to take ultrasounds, x-rays, EKG's and it took me a while to understand what happened. They moved me to a recovery room and I realized how in-depth the surgery was. I could hardly move. This was definitely worse than any other surgery I've ever had. I had Jackson-Pratt drains coming from my abdomen to take the pressure and swelling down. I couldn't move. I felt as if I had been hit by a truck.

After a few days, I was released and went home. I really wished at this point that I had family or friends close by. I had to jump back into life pretty quickly. Getting Taylor to school and picking her up was a struggle. I had to walk around with those drains hanging off of me for a week.

Christmas in the Hospital

Christmas was coming and we were struggling. Financially, mentally, and emotionally, we were worn out. Tim was working his butt off. His dirt school classes were keeping him busy on the weekends. The weekend before Christmas he got a call to do a huge private class for an "important" family in Orange County. It was scheduled by an assistant, and all we knew was it was going to be for three kids and two body guards. We were so curious! Maybe a movie star?

The class went great, and they paid Tim really well. They also tipped him really well. Turns out the wealthy family turned were the kids of the infamous Henry Nicholas, founder of Broadcom, who was sued and acquitted of profiting from insider trading. Still we were thankful for the business and it really made Christmas possible for us that year. I was able to help Tim with the class a little. I was pretty wiped out, and all I could do was get lunch and help with the paperwork, but I love helping him.

Christmas Eve day came and I was going downhill pretty quickly. I had worn myself out. I was weak and running a fever. Tim, Taylor, and I went out for breakfast and as I sat there waiting for my food, I decided that I should call the doctor. If I needed an antibiotic I needed to do it that day, or I would need to wait until the offices opened after the holiday. The doctor on-call demanded that I head to the Emergency Room immediately. Dang it! I knew that if I was running a fever I should have called earlier.

Friends Come Through

We called our friends, Doug and Glynis. Doug was able to come and get Taylor almost immediately. Taylor loved playing with their daughter, Kelly. They have been good friends to us throughout all of this. Very supportive and met us weekly for dinner. We kept them entertained by our crazy life updates. Everyone needs friends like this. On Christmas Eve, Doug was able to drop what he was doing, meet us to grab Taylor for a day of fun while we went to the ER.

We checked into Hoag Hospital and they knew we were coming. Before I knew it, we were moved to the back. I had my blood work done, IV started, everything. Even while I was being admitted to the hospital, I just couldn't believe that I was being admitted on Christmas Eve. I needed antibiotics and blood transfusions, my blood counts were way too low.

We hadn't had time to finish shopping. There were still a few things on Taylor's wish list. Shannon, Tim's daughter came into town and I encouraged Tim to leave the hospital and go with Shannon to grab the last few items. They looked, but couldn't find this one little toy Taylor really wanted. Jill Rein, one of his co-workers, ran around, found the toy, and bought it for Taylor. What an angel! We will never forget that act of kindness.

The floor nurse made our time in the hospital amazing for us. She brought in a Christmas tree from the nursing station made of Christmas balls. Our room was a private room with a spare bed, and it was cozy. Tim brought Taylor in, and she loved the tree. Our little room was perfect. Taylor had brought some Christmas artwork to help decorate the room. Everything was really cute. The transfusions started and the presents Tim brought from home were lined up against the wall. We were actually having a nice time.

It was an exciting Christmas on many levels'... My brother and his family traveled from Maui and had just gotten to my Mom's house to visit. They would be heading our way on Christmas day. I was so excited to see everyone. I was especially hoping my Mom and her husband Art C.

would be joining them. Since I have been sick and my Mom no longer is able to drive, I really don't get a chance to see her. The last few times have been very rough. Art C. and I have not seen eye to eye on her treatment. I totally understand where he was coming from. I can't say that if I were faced with Tim showing the beginning signs of Alzheimer's, I wouldn't have made exactly the same decisions at that time.

I have always known how much Art C. loved my Mom. He has been amazing to her since they have been together. I couldn't have handpicked someone who could have ever treated her better. For him she was a princess. She felt it, and that made a huge difference in her life. When she began to show signs of forgetting or getting lost, it was hard for her husband to accept. I would bring it up, and I was shut down time after time, until it became too difficult emotionally for me to be around them.

I did miss them and was very disappointed when they opted to stay home and not see me while I was in the hospital. It hurt my feelings, I felt that I could have very well died from my cancer, and they didn't take the time to come and see me. It felt terrible. The gifts were sent with Shannon and his family to give to our family. It was one more thing I had to swallow and put out of my head and my heart.

Old Wounds

I think in the back of my mind, my cancers were always an opportunity to bring me closer to my Mom and her husband Art C. But it always seemed as if it were an imposition. Like I was getting sick on purpose-for attention. I didn't do anything to deserve my cancers. I didn't ask for them. I didn't like them. I would have like to have used the opportunity to grow as a family. It was yet another painful revelation that nothing would or could ever change.

When my brother, Shannon, and the girls got to the hospital, it was so much fun to see all of the girl cousins hugging and jumping around. Taylor was beyond ecstatic. Since I knew well in advance they were coming, I had time to buy special gifts for each of the girls. It was a very happy time and a wonderful memory of family to lock in the vault.

The day after Christmas, it was back to work on getting me better. I had two more transfusions and a couple of CT scans. They found a mass in my kidney. A specialist was brought in and made the decision to biopsy the area while I was there. It looked very suspicious to them.

I was terrified. I honestly felt sick, like a sick, dying person. I had no energy, no zazzle, like I usually do. As they wheeled me into the room for the biopsy, I began to wonder if this was even worth the trouble. What would I do if the cancer had spread while I was on chemo? What could be done and was I willing to do it? I just didn't have the strength left to wrap my brain around it all. Just as I was beginning to feel hopeless, Tim walked around the corner with a Jamba Juice for me. I took a weak sip of the straw and I swear it was like liquid life. The more I drank, the better I felt.

During the biopsy, they were not able to grab any tissue from the mass. They opted to stop at that point, and I would follow up with the urologist when I was released. Slowly the blood transfusions were working. I started to feel alive again. My blood counts came up, and I was released a few days later.

I continued my chemo and followed up with the urologist. We did a scan and some ultrasounds over the next couple of months. As we had hoped it would, the mass turned out to be a cyst on my kidney and has not proven to be any of concern.

During this time, I had so much time to think about my life. About cancer and how it would affect my kids. The more I thought about everything, the more I knew I had to do something. I had always joked that I really would listen to God if he would just tell me what he wanted me to do. I didn't need to be hit over the head with the cancers. I came to realize that I did need to be hit over the head. I made several calls in one afternoon. The first one was to the American Cancer Society. I told them that I would love to talk about having cancer three times, and felt that I could help people. They took my info.

The next call I made changed my life dramatically. I called Myriad Genetics, the company that developed the BRCA test. I explained that I was BRCA positive and told them my story. I told them that I would do anything to help get this test into the knowledge-base of as many families as I could. I offered myself to them for anything I could do to make a difference.

About a month later, I got a phone call from Ogilvy Public Relations in New York City. They had been hired by Myriad to put together a speakers' training, and they were inviting me to travel to Salt Lake City and complete a speakers training. I was so excited! The day after I finished my last chemo, I was on a plane with Tim headed to Utah for a weekend training session.

I ended up being the first patient speaker for Myriad. I was flown to Montana to speak at a large medical center for the employees. It was a big deal. The higher-ups at Myriad also flew out for the event. I got up there, still bald from the chemo and told my story. This was the beginning of what I would do for the rest of my life.

Three of the patient speakers were chosen to do case studies that would be shared as marketing materials. Cynthia Kimball, Nancy Roemer, and me, were all asked and agreed to be featured as their case studies. Cynthia reached out to me when the studies were released and we formed a best friend bond quickly. I never was able to meet Nancy. She passed away shortly after the studies were out. We were devastated. This loss was a blow to all of us who were so dedicated to making sure that these hereditary cancers were being identified and treated successfully.

Cynthia and I met in person and have collaborated on many, many projects together. We have an energy that is incomparable, and together we are set on improving patient care, and how people can positively adapt to unplanned changes in their lives.

The Reconstruction: Putting it all back together again

In May of 2008 I was finally to the point where I could go forward with the double mastectomy and reconstruction. I was ready and excited. Dr, Curcio would be doing the double mastectomy. Dr. Kim would be doing a tram-flap reconstruction. This was an amazing concept for me. Taking the fat flap from my pregnancies which has shamed me my entire adult life and turning that shame into my new breasts was quite a revelation for me. Fortunately, everything worked out in my best interest. Doing implants were too risky. There was a chance the skin was too damaged from radiation to recover, and the chance of my body rejecting the implants was higher.

Enough said for me! One thing no one tells you about is when you are having reconstructive surgery is the planning and consultations. More directly…. The BEFORE pictures. YES! Before pictures. Flap and fat in full site of a camera. Boobs down where they shouldn't be. All of this is now part of my permanent record. Agggghhhh. The worst part isn't just knowing they were taken. It's having to look at them in living color. Talk about having to face reality.

Before I could have the surgery, I had to put down a pretty hefty deposit. I was sharing this with my long time friend Beth over lunch. We were commiserating together. At the end of the lunch as we were paying the bill. She handed me a check for the deposit. Friends can be there for you in so many ways. This was a huge testament to her love for me. I guess my boobs belong to Beth!

Beth and me.

I went in for the surgery. It went great-- nothing out of the ordinary. However, the pain was extreme. The amount of Jackson-Pratt drains hanging from my abdomen and new breasts was alarming. I had four of them across my lower abdomen, and two on each side at the breasts. This would prove to be a long recovery.

During my recovery, the area where the tram-flap was done wouldn't heal. Dr. Kim worked on it for months. I was speaking all over the country and this was becoming a real "stinking" pain! On the airplane one time, I could literally smell myself. I was changing the bandages a few times every day. By the time I got to the hotel, I was literally gagging. My wound was infected, and it was not getting any better.

When I got home I made yet another appointment with Dr. Kim. He decided that he was going to send me to the wound care center, to let them aid in the healing. When I met with Michelle, the physical therapist, I was mortified. The entire room smelled, and to measure how large the wound was, she had to stick her fingers into the wound. I can't begin to explain how humiliating it was. It was large! She introduced me to my new BFF, the wound vac. Yes, the portable vacuum that will be providing constant suction to the wound for the next three months. This was not a tiny machine. I had to wear it over my shoulder like a stinky air-putting handbag. I called it the farting machine. Yes, it smelled too. It was sucking the foul odor and substances that come with a huge infection and non-healing wound.

I was released from wound therapy on New Year's Eve of 2008. The wound had healed but with a horrible deep scar on the left side of my lower abdomen. So now Dr. Kim needed to go back and fix that. It really was unsightly, and had to be done. I was petrified to have another procedure, but I was assured this would be a small procedure compared to what I had already been through.

In June of 2009 when I met with Dr. Kim in the waiting area of the OR, he met with me and showed me where he was going to remove the scar. He also had talked about re-doing the belly button that he had created during the original surgery. I opted to leave it alone. I was happy with my new little belly button and really didn't think changing it was necessary. This was about a year after the double mastectomy and reconstruction. There was quite a bit of necrotic (dead) scar tissue on the right upper outer quadrant of the right breast that needed to be removed.

Dr. Curcio had already done a biopsy in the office, so we knew it was scar tissue. I really like my left breast and how he had shaped it. I asked if he could make the right one match the left one, since he was already working on the right side. He explained that he would need to change the left side to match the right side because the left side was bigger and fuller. I opted to leave it alone too. Enough was enough.

When I woke up from surgery I was sore but definitely not as bad as the one before. I did have a new Jackson-Pratt drain where the scar was revised in my abdomen. My breasts were wrapped tight. Seemed all was good, I was released and went home. When I got home and looked at the surgeries I was shocked. My belly button was redone and bandaged. I also had surgery on my left breast. I wasn't thrilled, but I figured it had already been done, so maybe it was the right thing to do. I was a little miffed, but I typically don't make issues about anything with people. Least of all, Dr. Kim, who was putting me back together like Humpty Dumpty.

During the surgeries, I thank God for my friend Morag and my "Girl Scout Moms". Morag organized meals for our family and picked Taylor up when we needed her to do so. Most of the time, Taylor spent the afterschool hours at the school's on-site after school program. Having a meal at home is something no one should ever overlook. A hot meal that you don't have to think about shopping for and fixing, is one of the biggest blessings of friends during a trying time.

When I woke up the next morning, my bed was soaking wet. Damn, my drain had leaked all of the fluid that it was collecting all night. I cleaned everything up and re-squeezed the drain balls. Hmmm, they wouldn't hold. I called and made an emergency appointment to see Dr. Kim. He wasn't there, so I met with his associate. I could bend over and you could hear the air puffing in and out of my abdomen. I physically showed him, bending back and forth making air noises each time. He assured me that everything was okay and could wait until Dr. Kim came back the following day.

I went home only to head back and meet with Dr. Kim the next morning. He took one look at the situation and scheduled me to go in for emergency surgery. I had an air leak. Air was seeping into my new wounds. The risk for infection was high. I went right over to the surgery center and went in for another surgery. When I woke up I could barely move. How could this be worse than before? My innards had been power washed. He had to remove any infection, or chance of it. He also removed my new belly button.

Okay, now I was kind of mad. When I went back for my post-op, I did question him as to why his associate didn't do anything. If it warranted an emergency surgery, you would think that would have been acknowledged and discussed the prior day. Dr. Kim swept it under the rug and said not to worry about it, that everything was okay. He also told me we could go in and re-do the belly button at a later date. HA! Never again would I go under the knife with him! For a year he had been screwing me up. He didn't send me to a wound specialist within the first few weeks of the wound not healing. From May through December I suffered with that. He re-did two body parts that I had opted not to do. I guess I signed blanket surgical repair consent. I am still not sure how the breast and the belly button were redone. I do know that Tim was there with me when I declined to have the two things redone.

It is now years later, and I still have no belly button. My left breast is a far cry from what is was. My breasts are quite disastrous. I am so afraid of going back in for repairs, I just suffer with my lopsided breasts and try not to let it bother me too much.

My Cancer Mommy

My Cancer Mommy book written by Taylor.

By this point everything went into a normal routine. I was speaking all over the country. My life was really, really good. I had no complaints. My love for God grew daily. My husband is a wonderful man and my best friend. My children are excellent and doing well. I started a non-profit organization called "Moms with Cancer," and I have been able to help countless moms all over the country. Some by just merely talking to them a few times, or sending out a mommy comfort-bag that includes a lot of essential hospital/chemo items. I also sent out the beautiful book Taylor wrote when she was only seven years old entitled "My Cancer Mommy." It tells the story of my cancer diagnosis, treatment and recovery, and of course, has a happy ending-all from a child's point of view.

When I had originally decided to do something with Taylor's thoughts and memories, I looked for a child who could draw some pictures to make a floppy little brochure to give away. I finally put an ad on Craigslist, which made it to Google search, where a young lady named Olga, from Barnaul, Russia read it. She responded with the most beautiful and amazing samples of her work. She was perfect! She also agreed to illustrate the book for free. She worked on the illustrations for a couple of months and each one she sent over was magic. What we thought would be a small brochure-type pamphlet, was slowly turning into a full color hard covered book. A REAL BOOK!!!

After the book was published, we had the illustrator of the book, Olga Matushkina, out to visit for a couple of weeks to show our gratitude to her for everything she did to make the book a reality. The book has proven to be such a helpful tool for so many children whose parent has been diagnosed with cancer. This young lady has been a huge blessing to myself and many, many people that she will never know. Her illustrations have helped give them hope. We took her everywhere a tourist would want to go; shopping, the beach, Catalina Island, and Disneyland, while we had our precious time with her.

One of her fondest memories was picking out our own strawberries at a local strawberry patch.

Moms with Cancer

In 2010, I crisscrossed the country speaking for Myriad Genetics. In Hawaii alone, I spent the equivalent of two months spaced out in one-week increments speaking. I traveled and talked. I was so proud of my life and what I was accomplishing. I knew I was making a difference and it made me proud--All from having this gene and cancer so many times. The one thing that was weighing heavily on me was getting Raquel tested for the gene. She was 26 years old, only three years younger than I was when I was diagnosed with my first breast cancer. She needed to be tested, and she refused. She was convinced that she would suffer the same fate as me. She was waiting like a ticking time bomb, ready to go off. Nothing I could say or do would convince her to test.

It was so important for all of us to know whether the children had inherited this gene from me. My Dad tested positive and my brother tested negative. Now all we had left were the children to test for the BRCA gene.

2010 was shaping up to be a very big year. We were planning a very large fundraising event for Moms with Cancer.org in May. The theme was a tea in a spring garden. A fellow patient of Dr. Curcio, Estela Riela, offered to put this huge event together for Moms with Cancer. I knew it would be fabulous, but I didn't know how involved I would be. It was all consuming. I was also very busy counseling Moms who were going through their diagnosis, treatments, and their own recoveries.

There were two Moms who affected me very personally from fall of 2009: Mary Martini, and Stephanie Guarascio. I have a lot of Moms across the country. While each one of them is special to me, I am able to keep a professional distance in order to protect myself from becoming too involved personally. These two ladies took me by storm. They were both petrified beyond anything I had ever seen.

Mary, a beautiful and sweet lady with so many questions. Yet she had no answers. She was diagnosed with metastatic cancer with no known primary. To not have the primary raises a lot of questions as to the correct way to treat her. She operated in panic mode. Searching for something, anything that could give her answers....or hope.

Her eyes always sparkled whenever I saw her. Her weight was dropping. No matter how much I encouraged her to eat what she wanted and keep eating, she would read articles on avoiding this and that and she took each of those bits seriously. She stopped all forms of sugar. Her weight plummeted. Now here she was, feeling terrible mentally, emotionally and physically. The one thing Mary enjoyed was eating chocolate and ice cream. She stopped eating sugar hoping this would be the step that helped to cure her cancer.

I would regularly get and make calls to Mary. She loved hearing my voice and said it always gave her hope. I am thankful for that; I loved talking to her and encouraging her. She was one of the sweetest women I had ever met. I met Mary's family and grew to love and enjoy each of them. Our families started having dinners together and just being there for each other. Tim was able to talk with Mary's husband, Nino, and give him some cancer husband advice. But mostly they talked about motorcycles and Nino's GPS business. Taylor made friends with their daughter Alyssa, and was able to play with her and spent a lot of time texting and talking to her.

Stephanie and me.

Stephanie Guarascio was recommended to me through Dr. Curcio. She had given their office permission to contact me, so I could call her. I did. Immediately there was a connection with this young mother of two small kids. Our conversations would last hours. We met face to face at Baby Beach in Dana Point so our girls could play and we could talk. It had been only a week after her diagnosis and Stephanie's world was upside down. Taylor and I got there a little early, and were anxiously waiting for them. Taylor just knew she was going to be meeting a new friend. I had no idea that I would be meeting a soul sister, a new best friend.

Stephanie and her kids walked up with the wind blowing in her long, thick, blond hair, her beautiful face beaming. Her clothes were absolutely beautiful and she shone. Her kids, Bella, 9, and Christian, 4, were also pure perfection. We sat down to talk, the kids played, and the time flew by. After that first meeting we both knew we had a very special bond and friendship that would last long beyond cancer.

Early 2010 found me emotionally and physically worn out. On top of caring for all of the Moms, I was traveling and speaking almost weekly. Add the fundraising event and all of the meetings and discussions that entailed, I was looking forward to the event being completed.

May moved on to us at a rapid pace. Before I knew it, I was pulling together the last minute program and all of the advertisements of support that had been given. Everything on the day of the event was truly a fairy tale. From the set up, until the very last moment of the event, magical would be a perfect word to use to describe it.

The weather was perfect. The garden that Estela chose was in full bloom and everything looked exceptional. The baskets for the silent auction lined the entire perimeter of the event, and were stunning. As the ladies began to show up in their spring attire and beautiful hats, the tone of the event was cheery, hopeful, and full of class. White umbrellas floated at the top of the blue skyline, overlooking the foothills of Orange County and the golf course.

The highlight for me, was being surprised by Mary Martini. She was asked to say a few words about me. I don't think I have ever been so honored. Even though she wasn't feeling well and she was nervous beyond belief, she got up in front of this very full audience and spoke so eloquently about having support from me and Moms with Cancer. I looked across the table as she spoke and saw the faces of Raquel and her boyfriend Loren. My eyes found Taylor in a cute dress, and looked out into the audience. I saw my handsome husband Tim, walking around in a tuxedo and sporty pink bow tie as an usher. Further away, I could see Jordan doing the photography for the event. I have never been more proud.

Chapter 7: Round 4

Down, But Not Out

I was worn out after the event. Normally, I don't get too tired. Physically, mentally, and emotionally I was exhausted. I figured with all of the traveling I was doing and working on the event, I had just overdone it. I was back to falling asleep in my car in parking lots because I couldn't stay awake. I went to my cardiologist and everything checked out okay. The only thing really bugging me was my abdomen. I went from doctor to doctor the rest of the year. On more than one occasion after complaining that my stomach was bloating out so badly, it was suggested that I contemplate a lap band surgery. The doctors said it would take the pressure off my abdominal area. The muscles from the tram-flap surgery were not holding everything in place.

I went in for a colonoscopy and endoscopy, I went for the lap band consultation and first appointment. I just sensed something was off and opted to not have the lap band. After all of the surgeries I had already had, I was not eager to have more surgery and endure more recovery time.

Genetic Testing My Family

Best of all, because of the event, and seeing how all of this affected me, and noting how important the testing was for my children, they all agreed to test. Taylor tested first. Then Jordan tested, and finally Raquel. When summer rolled around and Phillip came out, he also tested. Now at last, my entire family was tested, and we had the results.

I get a lot of questions about testing the two youngest kids. "How will knowing their results change their medical management before age 25?" "Why wouldn't you wait until they can make decisions for themselves?" Well, I answer each person with strong conviction. I watched Raquel suffer from the time she was 11 years old when I was diagnosed the first time. I remember looking at her sweet little face and seeing the fear that haunted her, "When would I get breast cancer?" She was convinced that she was just like me and it was only a matter of time. As her breasts were growing, they were a reminder, in her mind, that she would eventually suffer the same fate as me.

For me it was torture watching her make decisions based on a future she had already played out. How could I not test my family and give them concrete answers? In my experience, fear is the worst enemy. Not knowing the answer to questions can torture people into living lives that are not to their full potential. Testing my family was not an option; I had to do it.

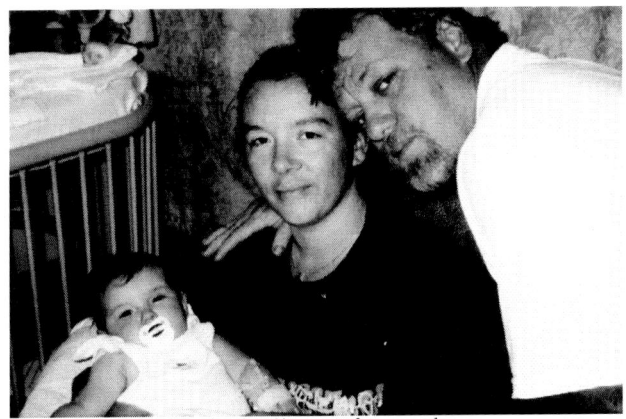

Maiya, Becca and my brother Shannon after a very long cancer surgery.

Before my kids tested, my Dad and brother tested first. Dad, as expected, was positive. My brother, Shannon was negative. This information was so important. Shannon has a beautiful little girl, Maiya. When Maiya was only six months old, she was diagnosed with a stage four neuroblastoma. My niece had cancer. She went through major surgeries and was not given much hope of surviving this cancer. Maiya's mom, Becca, and my brother would not hear of it. Little Maiya endured months of chemotherapy and constant medical follow ups. I am proud to say that she is a healthy, happy seven-year-old. To know that she did not carry the gene was glorious.

As for my own children, Raquel, Jordan and Taylor tested negative. Phillip tested positive. The BRCA gene is pretty concise. Each child of a mutation carrier has a 50% chance of inheriting the gene. That could have meant all of my kids could have tested positive. My friend, Cynthia Kimball, had this happen in her family. All five of the daughters inherited the gene from their father. Of the five, three have been diagnosed with early onset breast cancer. They have all had risk reducing surgeries.

When I told Raquel that her test was negative her first response was "I can have babies!" We were in tears. This revelation changed her life. I suddenly saw a beautiful confident young woman emerge. She has a lightness about her now that came from the knowledge that she was at the normal general population risk for cancer. For Phillip, he has a great role model in my Dad. At 67, he is in perfect health. The main concern for us with Phillip is passing the gene on to his children. Since he is only 18 I hope we have a long while before this is a topic we have to face. After doing some brief research, we do have a lot of hope that this gene will end with Phillip and he will be able to have healthy BRCA negative children.

My Sweet Mary

Nino, Alex, Mary, and Alyssa

In July my world fell apart. Mary Martini fell quite ill and we rallied around her and her family. There wasn't too much I could do except to be there for them and continue to give her hope. I am never short on hope. The Martini's lived over an hour away from us. When she got home from the hospital, we decided to meet them at their house and spend some time with them. I was shocked to see Mary. She was in her bed and not very coherent. She wouldn't drink anything and couldn't eat. She was skin and bones. I hopped onto the bed with her, and held her. I massaged lotion into her back and just tried to make her feel better. Tim and Nino were in the kitchen talking. Taylor and Alyssa were upstairs.

Mary struggled to get up and go to the bathroom. Nino and Tim went to the drug store and bought her a portable toilet. I continued to hold her and lightly massage her. I was able to coax her to drink a tiny bit of water.

It was getting late, so Tim and I said our goodbyes for the evening and took Taylor home. We chatted on the way home, and prayed for the Martini's. Just as we pulled in, my phone rang and it was Nino. He was very upset and said Mary was not responding at all. He called 911 and they came and took her to the emergency room. We hopped back in the car and headed back to Nino and Mary's.

By the time we got to the ER, they had started hydrating Mary with IV fluids. She looked so much better. She was complaining about the paramedics coming into her house and getting her, glancing over and giving Nino dirty looks. But she did agree to drink some soda and some water. Hope once again abounded. Mary's

Mom and Dad were flying in the next morning from Florida to stay with her and help her recover at home. Once Mary was stabilized, Tim and I went to their home, grabbed a couple of hours of sleep and then ran to the airport in San Diego to pick up Mary's parents, Al and Darlene.

We tried to explain to them what had been going on, that she was not doing great, but that she had improved since the night before. We really did our best to prepare them for what they would see. When we got to the hospital, Mary was expecting her Mom, but seeing her Dad was a total surprise. She was up and coherent. It was so good to see everyone together. They got Mary situated in a room. Just as she was settled in the hospital, the staff realized that she needed to be moved to a new hospital that was equipped to give her the chemotherapy she needed. Mary was in good spirits and laughing. We decided it was time for us to go home.

The next day was July 27, 2010. It was my son Jordan's 23rd birthday. We went back to see Mary and we were shocked to find that she had slipped into a coma shortly before we got there. They put her on a ventilator to help her breathe, but her organs had already begun shutting down. After much discussion with the family and doctors, they decided to remove the ventilator and let her go at her own pace.

Within minutes of removing the vent she took her last breath. All of us were surrounding her and I was praying out loud for her passing to be smooth. She was at peace and she was beautiful. I have never been a part of such a moving moment. My heart grew another part, and also at that moment it died a little bit too.

Mary's death had a profound effect on me. How could my senses have been so far off? How could I have had hope until the last minute that she would survive this and start a new healthy life? The only place I could turn was to God. Mary's faith was strong, and although she never accepted herself dying and fought until that very last breath, I know she is at peace smiling on her family and friends. I also know that she is sorely missed.

Back in the Ring

I tried to concentrate on slowing my lifestyle down but soon October, which is breast cancer awareness month, was upon me. My own health was declining and I was scared. I went to my internist and had a urinary tract infection. Antibiotics were prescribed and within a day, I did feel better…for a bit. I became congested and was having trouble breathing.

Dr. Curcio had sent me in for a breast MRI just as normal protocol. The test was torture. With a breast MRI you lay face down with your breasts hanging down in two holes. You are then backed, face down, on a bed with a tiny breathing hole into the MRI machine. Between the whirring and whishing of the machine, I had picked out a 'Mercy Me' CD to listen to and hearing them singing to me about God made the hour a bit more bearable.

By the time it was over, I was dripping wet with sweat and couldn't breathe. I had to just sit there until my breathing normalized. I went into the changing room to get dressed. When I looked into the mirror, I was horrified. There were two large red rings around my breasts and my abdomen was protruding out. I grabbed my cell phone camera and took pictures. I was in pain, and I was disgusted with how I looked and felt.

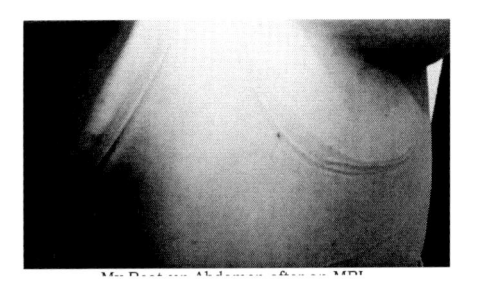

A week later I got a call from Dr. Curcio's office. The breasts looked fine but more concerning was a "prominent pleural effusion". WHAT???? I had never heard of this. I had to write it down. I needed to call my cardiologist, Dr. Bruss and internist, Dr. Pham right away. I called both doctors offices and made appointments. Dr. Pham's office had me come in right away. I was scheduled to speak in St. George, Utah and I was leaving the next day, Saturday. Dr. Pham ordered antibiotics. I asked him if I could go on this trip. He conceded, knowing how important it was to me. He was worried about a pulmonary embolism so he told me to be sure I knew where the emergency rooms were. During this appointment Dr. Bruss returned my call. He had an appointment set up for me a week from Tuesday to see a pulmonologist to have the effusion drained. Which meant I had to have my lung tapped. Yikes. No way!!! A needle into my back between the ribs to remove this fluid. But he, too, agreed that if speaking made me happy and feel good, then I could go ahead with the trip.

Tim and me in Utah.

The trip was amazing. Tim and Taylor drove up with me and we made it a mini family vacation. I bought so many decongestants and cough medicine just to keep me breathing. We stopped in Las Vegas on the way up and did a little sightseeing. I was having a tough time breathing and it was apparent. We continued on, we were having a good time. We made it into Utah and the St. George area was incredible. The hosts of the event were so gracious and I had a blast at the event.

We drove up to Bryce Canyon and on to Zion National Park in Utah. There were some amazing sights. I wish I had been feeling better to fully enjoy them. The higher in elevation we got, the more difficult it became to breathe. On the way home we stopped in Las Vegas and met up with Tim's daughters, Karen and

Shannon. The next day we all headed to meet up with Laura, the oldest, so the girls could go to their Mom's for Thanksgiving.

Choking on my fluids

When we got back home my breathing was more difficult. I held out as long as I could, but on the Saturday after Thanksgiving I finally asked Tim to take me to the emergency room. There was no way I could make it until Tuesday to see the pulmonologist. I guess I looked pretty bad because they took me right into the back and put me on oxygen, took x-rays and called in a specialist to tap my lung right away. Morag came and picked Taylor up for us. I can't explain the fear that was running through me. They were going to put a needle into the right side of my back between my ribs and pull out the fluid. I was going to have to be awake and positioned sitting up and hunched over.

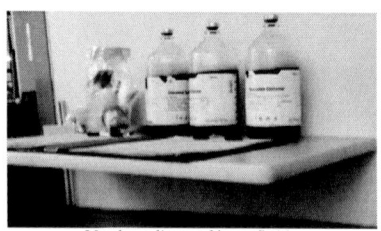

My three liters of lung fluid.

The doctor numbed the area and then inserted the needle. The needle drained fluid into liter sized bottles. Three of them full of fluid! My collapsed lung began to sting and hurt as it filled up with air. I must say that by the time I got back into my ER holding area. I felt 100% better. I could breathe!!!

It was kind of weird in my holding area. They brought the three large glass containers filled with the amber liquid they had just retrieved from my body and placed them on my bedside table. It reminded me of having a baby and they bring the precious bundle to your room. They didn't know what to do with it, what tests they needed to order. Several doctors came by, and they finally got ahold of a medical oncologist who told them what tests to order on my fluid. I was still scheduled to see the pulmonologist on Tuesday, so we left the ER and I went home feeling much better.

I hadn't felt this good in a very long time. I called the pulmonologists office to confirm that I should still come in. I wasn't sure what we were going to do but they said yes. Tim and I went over and waited for about two hours until we got in to see the doctor. Our spirits were really high and I felt good. We were laughing and giggling together while we waited for the doctor.

When he came in there really wasn't too much he could tell us. He excused himself and went to see if there were any last minute results he could get to share with us.

A few minutes later he returned and he started by saying, "I know you think this visit was a waste of your time." We never had even thought that, nor did it cross our minds. "Mrs. Rice, you have cancer." I felt as if someone had simultaneously sucked every ounce of air out of me AND punched me very hard in the stomach. I could feel my insides starting to flush and the tears were reaching my eyes. He showed us the results that had been faxed over. Sure enough, positive. The lung fluid had come back as carcinoma. I excused myself to go to the restroom where I stood there with a tears spilling down my cheeks.

A fear overcame me. Four times. Four times, how could my body handle cancer for a fourth time? I headed slowly back to the office, I could hear my heels clicking on the hard concrete floors. As I walked in the Doctor and Tim were making appointments for CT scans and blood work. I looked at the orders and it said lung cancer as the diagnosis. I looked at the doctor and asked a question I have never asked before, "Can I make it?" He just smiled at me and said he was sorry that this was a really bad time of year for this to happen.

I held my head up as high as I could and began to walk to the car with this new sentence hanging over me. I called Dr. Curcio and I cried. She was even more shocked to hear the diagnosis and of course would be there for whatever I needed. Our next stop was to the Women's Cancer Research Foundation's office in Newport Beach where Dr. Brown, my gynecologic-oncologist worked. I spoke to Carlina who is the Executive Director. She called in Katrina who is in charge of clinical trials and studies. They worked so quickly to get me in and seen. By the end of the day, I had an appointment set up with Dr. Brown for the following day.

When we got home, the first thing I did was go to the internet and type in four time cancer survivors. Then five time cancer survivors. They were there. I had hope. There are so many times I wish I could call my Mom and talk to her. The more she is taken over by Alzheimer's, the more I wanted her back and to have a mother-daughter re-do.

It was definitely a metastasis from my fallopian tube and not the breast. It wasn't lung cancer. So I made the necessary appointments to have a port-a-catheter placed into my chest to get more chemotherapy. Friday, I would go in for that surgery. Monday, I would start chemo. Wow, this was quick action and I was thankful.

A huge prayer movement was put into place. Everyone that I knew from all over the country and beyond, had me in prayer chains. I was being prayed for daily in the thousands. During all of this, although I was scared, and Tim and I had conversations that we didn't want to have, I was so at peace with what was happening. I never felt a sense of hopelessness. Nor did I have a sense of being alone. I was never alone in my mind, body or spirit. I felt the presence of God and all of the prayers that were being said to bless me.

My port-a-catheter placement wasn't as easy as the one prior. For this one, they kept me awake. When I came out in recovery, my neck was in pain. I had two incisions, one was in my neck the other was down lower on my chest. My neck was tight and swollen. The catheter was, and still is, very tight and irritating.

Monday, I went in for my appointment with Dr. Brown's office for chemo. They placed the IV needle into my new incision. I do prefer this over the traditional form of finding a vein on my hand or wrist to start the IV. One quick poke and it is in. The first chemo was done with no problems. We decided that I would break one round of chemo into three one-week sessions with the fourth week off. The first week would be the Carboplatin and Taxol, and the next two weeks would be Taxol only. I can't believe what a difference this made for me. Although I wasn't thrilled with going in every week, however, the weekly doses were better tolerated and seemed to do a better job in clinical studies.

After the first round, we went in and consulted with a medical oncologist, Dr. Minh Nyguen, a young advanced doctor. He was the one who ordered the tests for me when I had my lung tapped six weeks earlier. We went in to talk to him and see what his thoughts were on any new medications and what he would use. He went over all of the results from the scans that were just coming in. We were shocked. The tumors were all over my abdominal area. One in my lower right side was the size of an orange. There were many more scattered throughout my body up into my sub-clavicle lymph nodes. This wasn't looking good. My CA125 blood test was at an extremely elevated high of 1,750. The normal level for a CA125 is below 20. We decided that we would continue to see both Dr. Brown and Dr. Nyguen.

This cancer was different than the others. I couldn't control my body. First the fluid in my lungs. Then the urine. I couldn't control my bladder and on many occasions I wet myself. The tumors were pushing on my bladder and my colon. The chemo was giving me diarrhea and Tim had to help clean me up. I have never felt such humiliation. My body was out of my control. I was scared.

After two doses of the Carboplatin I had a reaction. I was sitting with Tim and they had just told me to let them know if I felt sick or anything unusual. I hate to complain. When I started feeling nauseated, I asked Tim to run downstairs and grab me something to munch on. I was sure it was from the chemo pre-meds. Just as he left, I tried to get up to go to the bathroom and I literally couldn't move. I was starting to pass out. I got the nurses attention just as I broke out into a sweat and things started to blur. They went into action. I was given a medication to counteract the reaction and within 20 minutes I felt like I had been beat up, but not too bad. The nurses joked with me that this was not the way to get the paramedics to come in and visit us! Tim came back during the middle of all this and it scared him to death.

After that episode, Dr. Brown didn't want to do any more Carboplatin on me, and we still had the de-bulking surgery and lymph node dissection to do. Since we were changing chemo drugs and giving me a three week break, now was a great time to have the surgery done.

My CA125 was responding and dropping. That was good news. Dr. Nguyen was in agreement with Dr. Brown on the medications, but wasn't sure that the surgery was completely necessary at this point. He did order scans so I could see how the tumors were doing. This was a good middle ground for me. I really needed to know if they had responded to the few doses of chemo I had already had, or if they weren't affecting the cancer at all. I trusted Dr. Brown, and if he thought doing surgery was the way to go, after the scans came back, then I would do what he recommended. He was, after all, a top gynecologic/oncology surgeon and had saved many women's lives. I had two doctors I trusted and I felt in good hands.

The scans came back and we were all amazed by how much the chemo had shrunk the tumors. Before surgery there were only a few we could see. My CA 125 continued to fall. To all of us this was miraculous news. I knew God was working a miracle and I wasn't going to let anyone down. My hope was eternal.

Dr. Brown scheduled me for surgery and it was flawless. While I woke up sore and stapled, I knew I was on the road to being healed.

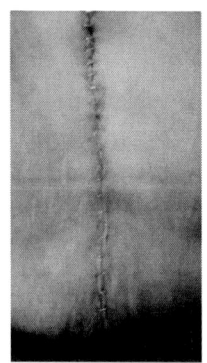

My de-bulking staples post surgery.

My chemotherapy continued and there have been trying weeks. A lot of the time my face turned very red, and I was nauseated from the drugs. I was coming to the end of my six months of scheduled chemo. Like clockwork, I did just as I was told. There were no more surprises in my treatment, and for the most part, short of the fatigue, I felt really good. For me, the third and fourth days after chemo were my down days. The steroids did a great job of giving me the sense of energy and vitality, which always translates to me feeling good and powerful.

Morag and me.

I can't thank my friend Morag enough. She has been there every minute of every day for me. Whenever I needed help with Taylor, she was there. She never complained or made me feel like a pain. There is not a lot of glory in being the side kick of the sick chick, but I thank God for her every day. She has been with me now through two cancer battles. Helping in ways she will never know. My gratitude is boundless for her and the friendship we have grown into will last a lifetime. Everyone needs to have their own personal angel. She didn't go overboard and baby me, she treated me as a normal friend. She was always there when I needed her. Who can ask for more?

I started to do a little speaking and traveling towards the end of my treatments. It felt good to be back in the saddle so to speak, but as much as my heart was into it, my body was screaming for me to stop and recover. I had a false sense of energy. When the chemo was finished, so were the steroids. I know that at the completion of chemo there is always a down period of time where I have a feeling of loss and don't really know what to do or how everything will be. The end of this chemo was particularly hard. I crashed. Over the next two months, each day I became more depressed. I was sleeping as much as I could, and oddly enough, my hope was dashing. Here I was cancer free again and I was depressed.

It got so bad that I had to reach out to Dr. Curcio, Stephanie and of course Morag. I analyzed myself into oblivion. But during those analyses I remembered that I had been given steroids every single week with my chemo. The feeling the steroids gave me was a false sense of energy, which I mistakenly took for real energy. When I stopped the steroids I dropped hard, emotionally and physically. As soon as I figured that out I felt better.

Life once again became "normal." Stephanie and I both needed to be involved in something and we both needed to earn some money. We started a little jewelry company called "Happiness in a Bag." Together we do jewelry shows and have a blast working together.

Our girls are great friends and Stephanie and I share a history of cancer and a future of hope. Tim and her husband, Chris, have become great friends too. We have become a great little extended family.

We can always talk about cancer or the aches and pains that no one else wants to listen to now that we are "healed." The fear remains with each ache and pain.

Chapter 8: Round 5

My Palooka Cancer
(Palooka= lousy boxer who usually looses fight in 4-6 rounds.)

Early this year (2012), my CA125 began to slowly rise. Each month it was doubling. In March Dr. Brown and I decided to begin chemotherapy again. When it reached 100, I started a regimen of weekly Taxol. It was very discouraging. Five times. Five times. Five times. Cancer for the fifth time.

Major Loss

A month after I started my chemo, I got the phone call I was dreading. My caller ID had already told me what I was about to hear. My Mom had passed away. It wasn't unexpected, but it was devastating. Tim and I jumped into the car and drove two hours to get to the home she was living in to try and see her and say good-bye. We made it. I have never seen anything so sad and sobering as seeing my Mom laying in her bed lifeless. During the times I was able to visit her I learned to love her again. She was my Mommy. She had lost so much weight she looked like a little hummingbird. I cried for so long. I just couldn't stop. I cried for the loss of her, I cried for all of the time we lost and the time we would never have. The loss of a parent is what I have been fighting to prevent my own children from having to experience; now it was my brother Shannon and I who were saying our good-byes.

After three-four-week rounds of Taxol my CA125 levels kept increasing to over 300. Dr. Brown switched my chemo to Avastin. I used Avastin for months and showed no response. You never know how medicine will work until you try it. There is a huge difference between the two drugs and how they work. The Taxol caused me to lose my hair AGAIN. The Avastin does not cause hair loss and thankfully my hair is beginning to sprout. Gray. Ugh. So thin and light. My scalp is very visible, but I really don't care. No hats or wigs for me. But, I do have to say that Miss Clairol has once again become a dear friend! I am now on a chemotherapy called Topotekan. It has only been two weeks and we will do a blood check in a week to see if this one is working.

I pass what Dr. Brown calls "The Normal Test." If you saw me in a grocery store, you wouldn't know anything was happening with my health. I feel bad the first week of chemo, which is three consecutive days. Then I slowly bounce back to feeling great. This cycle will continue until we obliterate this cancer or we find a new chemotherapy that works better or has less side effects.

Nutrition and Living

I really had to start thinking about what was triggering my cancers. Dr. Curcio called me and wanted me to start taking Low Dose Naltrexone. She also talked to me about diet. The main vice that I had and knew was not good for me was Diet Coke. Especially in the quantities I drank. If that was a trigger I knew it would have to go. I felt like a junkie giving up a very addictive drug. It took me a few weeks of "suffering" but I finally did it. I started drinking sparkling water with a little lime in it. I never thought I would like that, but now I look forward to it.

My diet was next. I have always been a pretty healthy eater. No dairy, back from the Mary Lou Henner diet days. No red meat, courtesy of a disgusting 20/20 report 20 years ago. No pork, thanks to my Dad butchering my pet pig "Choo Choo Baby" and trying to get me to eat her. I hate fish and everything to do with seafood. Even though I know how good it can be for you, I just can't bring myself to eat it. For a long portion of my life I was vegan. But I wasn't healthy, clearly. I ate too many carbohydrates. That was another major addiction. I'm still working on it, but I am about 90% there.

I have read almost every book on cancer diets and some were so extreme. Now after my fifth cancer nothing is too extreme. I am Facebook friends with a lady named Elaine Cantin. She has been very helpful to many people with cancer. She shared her diet that she designed and it has literally changed the outcomes of hundreds (at least) of people's cancer. I love her new book, "The Cantin Diet".

I have been following her regimen pretty faithfully. Then the next time I did my blood count it dropped by 2/3's. The next three weeks I only partially did it. I was traveling and speaking, so I dropped the ball and my blood counts dropped only 6 points. I am now back on her low carb-based diet and feeling good. I eat as organic as I can, but I am getting better. I now actually love kale salads.

I will never doubt the power of diet and health. I have seen it for myself and I am a believer. First and foremost, I still believe that anyone diagnosed with cancer needs to keep eating. As they say Mangia, mangia! Now I say eat as healthy as you can. Everyday is a new day. Everyday you make a goal to eat right, and do it over and over again.

Chapter 9: Unanimous Decision

Your Happiness at Stake

Okay, I think I have shared my fears, my innermost thoughts and my most shameful times. Now that you know me pretty well, we're going to get to the real reason for this book. "Thriving." As you know, I barely survived. Most of the time I battled myself on whether I even wanted to.

I thank God for thwarting every effort I made to give up. I have always had a deep relationship with God. Although I loved God, I didn't understand what my life was about. I didn't have any idea why I had to go through the things that piled up on me. I know I personally have responsibility for the crappy decisions I made; my life has been extreme. It embarrasses me when I have to recount all of the things I have shared with you. So with that said, not too many people know everything about me. I usually pick and choose what I am going to reveal, and to whom.

It never has to do with whom I'm speaking to. It always has to do with where I am in my life, where I am in my growth, what I'm learning to accept, and fully digest as a part of who I am, and WHY.

I have learned to balance my spiritual God-loving self and me, DeAnna the one I hold accountable and sometimes misunderstood, or even disliked, person. I have learned that not all things are black or white. Wrong or right. They just are. They just are.

It has always been hard for me to not have a specific reason for why something happened or why somebody did something. One great lesson I have learned is sometimes that's just the way it is. To continue searching for all of the whys to things that really don't matter, is giving up your current opportunity to live and enjoy life.

Chapter 10: Going the Distance

Here are my secrets......
DeAnna's 7 Steps to Happiness

1. Choose to be happy.
"Most people are about as happy as they make up their minds to be."
- Abraham Lincoln

This is not a new problem for people caught up in a life that is moving too fast. With electronic everything and offers from businesses to do everything we don't want to do or think we don't have time to do, from cleaning our house to picking up our dog's poop. We have too many decisions and choices running through our heads. Knowing that the Happiness Factor has been an issue for probably all of mankind we have learned one secret truth that works! Choice.

CHOOSE TO BE HAPPY. Through everything that has happened in my life, people always ask how I continue to smile. That's easy! I don't allow myself to think about everything that has gone wrong, is wrong, or can go wrong. I don't live day-to-day thinking about the what-ifs. I just live. I enjoy each day, and I judge things in clumps of time. My son just turned 18. This is a major milestone. He was only seven months old when this battle started. 18 years!!! Yay me!

2. Know what makes you happy.
"Unhappiness is not knowing what we want and killing ourselves to get it."
- Don Herald

It's hard to be happy if you haven't thought realistically about what really makes you happy. It's really easy to get depressed when we begin judging our lives and comparing them to others. We need to stop and take toll of what we truly love and value.

Some of my examples are my kids, the ocean, boating, koi fishponds, flowers, horses, a clean organized home, and music. Make your own list and cut out pictures. Once we can visualize what makes us happy and feel how we feel inside when we think about them, we know we are on the right track.

3. Learn to accept that you alone are responsible for your level of happiness.
"The best years of your life are the ones in which you decide your problems are your own. You do not blame them on your Mother, the ecology, or the President. You realize that you control your own destiny." - Albert Ellis

This can be a tough one. But I have to say it is the most freeing concept. We all have a person or people that have screwed us. Some horrifically...some just annoyingly, yet we will hold on to these actions and let them determine our outlook, and therefore our happiness level.

As for our parents, they are often the biggest offenders in our minds...And don't be surprised when you find out that no matter how hard you tried to be a different kind of parent and to give your kids the things that you wanted or that would have made you happy, you too will likely be at the top of their list.

Some of us were blessed with loving parents, some of us got distant parents, some simply got abusive or crappy parents. You are not your parents and you are not a child. You have to make the decision to choose to be happy, regardless of how you were raised. Your parents have no control on your thoughts, actions, and how you respond today to issues that arise in your life.

Letting go doesn't mean that you are accepting or condoning what you feel someone has done to you. It means understanding that while there are truly mean, sick people, out there, most of us are just not aware of the power we have to hurt others. As I go through my life, I really believe that the majority of people in life are doing the best they can, with what they know. Does it mean it's okay? No. But it does give you permission to live your life freely. Don't focus on things that people have said or done to you, and let them control your future.

4. Gratitude
"We tend to forget that happiness doesn't come as a result of getting something we don't have, but rather of recognizing and appreciating what we do have."
– Frederick Koenig

Learning to be grateful can be an exercise in strength. Especially when you are being tested, when things are falling apart and all you can feel is the deep dark pit in your stomach. Being grateful is the gift you give to yourself. It is the thankfulness you give to God.

Start with the small things that you can take for granted. A good parking space. A stranger smiling at you. A phone call from a friend at just the moment you needed it. I promise you that when you start looking for things to be grateful, they show up in abundance.

5. Recognition

"In order to have great happiness you have to have great pain and unhappiness... otherwise how would you know when you are happy?"
-Leslie Caron

This is one that is so powerful when we are ready to grasp and fully understand it. People ask me all the time "How can you be happy all of the time with everything you go through?" My favorite has always been something that more than one person has said to me…"When I think my life is bad, I always think about you."

In order to truly appreciate what you have, you have to have known loss, pain, and some degree of unhappiness. When I talk to other cancer patients, especially those being diagnosed for a second or third time, I look them in the eye and tell them a truth that is so real to me. "You have been given a great blessing. You have been given something that most people never have to experience.

"You now have the ability to have true empathy. Your life will never be the same. You have a choice from this moment on. You can choose to be angry that this has happened to you, or to choose a life of acceptance, happiness and love."

6. Worry
"Worry doesn't help tomorrow's problems, but it does ruin today's happiness."
-Anonymous

The biggest happiness sucker out there is worry. Worry has the ability to destroy your happiness, your friends, and your family. Worry is the battle of your mind trying to fix a problem that is beyond your control. Let me emphasize "Worry is trying to solve something that is beyond your control."

A good habit to practice is "If you can change what's bothering you, change it." This sometimes means facing a fear or taking an action that is difficult. However worrying day after day sucks the life and spirit out of you. If you can change it or fix it, do it. On the other hand if it is a situation you have no control over and there is nothing you can do to change it, you have to let it go. Every spiritual and religious thought group believes this.
Let it go. It is what it is.

7. Perfection
"Being happy doesn't mean that everything is perfect. It means you've decided to look beyond the imperfections." –Unknown

Happiness doesn't exist to the extent of "perfection." I like things to be the best they can be. I hate mediocrity. But it has to be within our realm of happiness. When we understand what makes us happy and what happiness is to us, it makes it easier to make decisions, to worry less and to stick to our happiness goals.

The idea of perfection is chasing something that is constantly changing. We need to be so specific in our idea of happiness. It's then that you will know when you have reached your goal. It doesn't mean give up after that, it means setting new goals. Don't keep chasing after something that won't really bring you authentic true happiness.

My Conclusion of Happiness

"Some pursue happiness, others create it."
– Anonymous

When you wake up every morning and choose happiness you are literally creating happiness. It is impossible to be unhappy long term, when you are in the business of creating your own happiness. In the short term, when you train yourself to believe in happiness, it is like a game to find happiness even in the darkest of hours. When even the most terrible situations are underway, you can find something positive. It may take hours, days, or even longer. If you begin to look for the good, for the jewel in the ruins, you will begin to live the life you dream of.

Satisfaction wells up from deep within you. It actually becomes difficult to stay sad or unhappy. I'm not saying that everyday will be walking in a field of dreams, or that you won't experience sadness or anger. You will just learn to control your reaction, and more importantly your "bounce back" time. Resilience becomes second nature. The more you learn to turn your problems over to God, yes, surrender and trust, the happier and more joyful you will become. It is a natural part of God's promise.

God is a good, loving God, and I know that during my moments of weakness, of pain and confusion, it is God who is carrying me. Broken and hopeful. The more often he has carried me, the easier it is to know that I am God's miracle, and I will always be perfect in his eyes.

Wherever you are in your life path, please take a moment.
Close your eyes and reaffirm your beliefs. Repeat that You are God's miracle and you are always perfect in his eyes.

"Happiness is not the absence of problems but the ability to deal with them."
- Anonymous

DeAnna Rice / FIGHT LIKE A MOM/ 202

My Scrapbook

My Raquel and me.

Raquel and Jordan 1988.

Taylor, Lauren and Phillip.

My Mom and Taylor taking a dip.

10 year high school reunion.

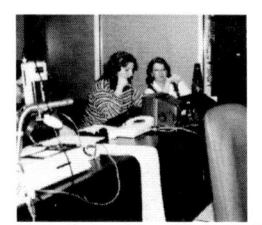

A coworker and I working on a TV show.

Me editing a television program.

DeAnna Rice / FIGHT LIKE A MOM/ 203

DeAnna, Tim, Laura and Taylor at Supercross.

Our daughters Karen, Laura and Shannon.

My childhood friend Gina...XOXO

Jordan and Phillip riding as Taylor and I watch.

Godmother Sharmane at Taylor's Christening.

Taylor and me at Seaworld.

The happy family and Taylor's 8th birthday.

My friend "Ned" and pure joy

Phillip and Jordan playing in North Carolina.

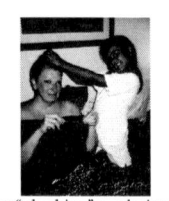

Taylor "plucking" my hair out.

Tim and I.

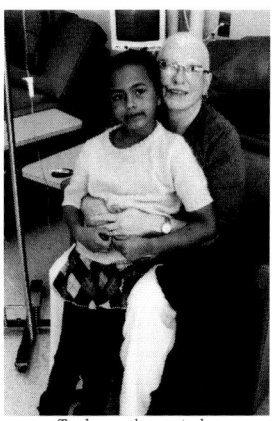

Taylor and me at chemo.

DeAnna Rice / FIGHT LIKE A MOM / 206

Tim, me, Raquel, Taylor and Lauren at Catalina.

Taylor's first dance recital with her biggest fan Phillip.

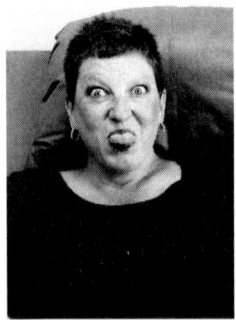

The real me during chemo!

Yet, another hairdo.

My mom and Taylor

My mom (Nana) helps Taylor ride.

Phillip, Laura and Taylor

He loves me!

About the Author

DeAnna Rice is a survivor and a thriver. She is on a mission to help everyone find their happiness. No matter what life throws at you, YOU can be happy.

Living proof and defeating the odds. DeAnna's life is one of tragedy and triumph, failure and redemption.

She lives in Laguna Hills, CA with her husband Tim and daughter Taylor. Their other children have grown and are scattered across the United States. They currently have two dogs and are enjoying the life that they have grown into.

A Special Tribute from Jordan:

Battling the odds...

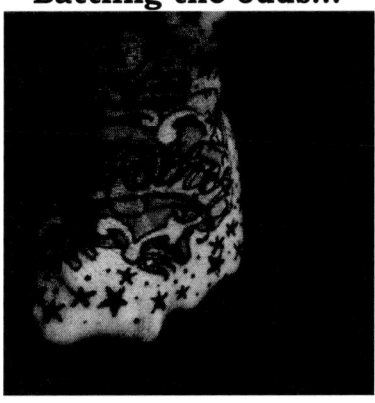

Mom:
I've watched you overcome and
fighting the odds many times.
I see you rise above while many give up.
I can't always tell you I'm proud of you everyday,
but, everyday I proudly wear your
name upon my hand forever.

Life hasn't been easy for you,
but, I see you stand up
each time ready for the next round.
You have nothing to prove to anyone, ever,
because we already admire your relentless efforts
to never quit.
You taught me that nothing stands in our way.

Thank you for fighting for the countless people out
there that look to you.
Thank you for teaching me to always live everyday
and reach for the sky.
I love you and I'm always proud of you.
    - Your son Jordan

Glossary of Terms

The following are terms you may hear or read while educating yourself about breast cancer health or dealing with breast cancer. This is not a complete list of medical terms. If you have any questions about terms not listed here, ask your healthcare provider.

Alternative therapies: therapies not necessarily proven by scientific studies such as use of nutritional supplements.

Adjuvant therapy: treatment given in addition to surgery, such as radiation therapy, chemotherapy or hormonal therapy.

Anemia: a decreased number of red blood cells, which may cause fatigue.

Anesthesia: drugs given before and during surgery so as not to feel discomfort.

Antiemetics: medicines that prevent or control nausea and vomiting.

Antiestrogen: a substance that blocks the effects of estrogen on tumors. Antiestrogens are used to treat breast cancers that depend on estrogen for growth: i.e. Tamoxofin

Areola: the circular area around the nipple of the breast. The areola is typically darker than the rest of the breast.

Aspiration: fluid is drawn from a cyst with a needle and syringe.

Axilla: the area under your arm, or armpit.

Axillary lymph nodes: the lymph nodes in the armpit.

Axillary lymph node dissection: surgery to remove some of the lymph nodes from the armpit.

Benign: a growth that is NOT cancerous.

Biologic therapy: cancer treatment that works by targeting specific cellular flaws associated with cancer cell growth.

Biopsy: removal of a tissue sample for examination under a microscope to see if cancer is present.

Bone marrow transplant: cells removed from the patient's bone marrow and given back after receiving high doses of chemotherapy.

Bone scan: an x-ray used to detect possible bone metastasis.

Breast conserving surgery: a portion of the breast is removed by either lumpectomy or partial mastectomy, usually followed by radiation therapy.

Breast reconstruction: surgery to rebuild a breast after mastectomy with either implants or tissue from another part of the body.

Breast self examination (BSE): examination of one's breasts for changes. Any change detected should be brought to the attention of a healthcare provider.

Calcifications: calcium deposits in the breast, which can be benign or malignant.

Carcinoma in situ:
DCIS- cancer that remains within the walls of the duct.
LCIS- is a non-invasive growth limited to the milk lobules. It is NOT cancer, but is a warning sign of increased risk of developing breast cancer.

CEA: Carcinoembryonic antigen: a blood test to determine if treatment is effective. Not used for screening.

Chemotherapy: treatment with drugs to destroy cancer cells.

Complementary treatment: therapies such as acupuncture, visualization, meditation, Tai Chi, and yoga, used in addition to traditional Western treatment.

Clinical Breast Examination (CBE): breast examination by a medical professional.

Clinical trials: research studies that test new drugs or procedures on patients to compare current standard treatments.

CAT SCAN (Computer Axial Tomography Scan): a scan in which multiple x-rays are taken of all or part of the body to produce an image of internal organs. Except for the injection of a dye, needed in some but not all cases, this is a painless procedure.

Core biopsy: removal of a piece of tissue with a needle, which is examined under a microscope to see if cancer cells are present. The patient is given a local anesthetic before a core biopsy is done.

Cyst: a fluid-filled mass that is usually benign. The fluid can be removed for analysis.

Ductal carcinoma: cancer found in the ducts and tissue of the breast.

Ducts: channels in the breast that carry milk to the nipple.

Estrogen: a female hormone produced primarily by the ovaries, and in small amounts by the adrenal gland. Estrogen may promote the growth of cancer cells.

Excisional biopsy: surgery to remove a tumor or mass studied under a microscope to see if cancer cells are present.

Fibroadenoma: a type of benign breast tumor composed of fibrous and glandular tissue. These usually occur in young women.

Fibrocystic breast: a term used to describe various benign breast conditions.

Fine needle aspiration: a type of biopsy in which cells are removed using a needle and syringe. The cells are studied under a microscope to see if cancer is present.

Genetic risk counseling and testing: a method to determine an individual's risk of disease by examining the history and genetic material of the family. Genetic testing usually involves a blood or sputum test.

Healthcare team: a group of different health professionals who provide care and service to the patient.

Her-2/neu: a gene that produces a type of receptor that promotes cell growth with too many Her-2/neu receptors tend to be fast growing.

Hormone therapy: treatment of cancer by removing, blocking, or adding hormones.

Hospice: supportive care not to extend life, but to control symptoms and to improve the quality of life of a patient in the end stage of the disease. Hospice care is usually provided in the patient's home.

Hyperplasia: abnormal increase in the number of cells in tissue. It is a benign condition.

Imaging: technology to produce pictures of the inside of the body, including mammogram, ultra-sound, CAT scan, MRI and X-ray.

Implant: a silicone or saline-filled sac inserted under the chest muscle to restore breast shape after mastectomy.

Inflammatory breast cancer: an aggressive form of breast cancer that causes the breast to appear reddened and swollen, resembling a rash or infection; accounts for only 1% of breast cancer.

Invasive cancer: cancer that has spread from the duct or the lobe into surrounding tissue in the breast.

Latissimus Dorsi Flap: a type of reconstruction done after mastectomy, using muscle and skin from the back.

Lobular carcinoma: cancer that forms in the lobules of the breast.

Lobules: milk-producing glands within the breast.

Localized breast cancer: cancer that is confined to the breast.

Lumpectomy: surgery to remove a breast tumor and a small amount of surrounding tissue.

Lymphedema: swelling of the arm and hand caused by excess fluid that collects after lymph nodes are removed by surgery or after radiation treatment.

Lymphatic system: tissue and organs that produce and store lymphocytes, and the channels that carry the lymph fluids.

Lymph nodes: small structures throughout the body that filter out and destroy bacteria and toxic substances. The lymph nodes are connected by a system of vessels called lymphatics. The lymph nodes can collect cancer cells.

MRI (magnetic resonance imaging): an imaging technique that uses a powerful magnet to transmit radio waves through the body. The images appear on a computer screen as well as on film. The procedure is painless.

Malignant: cancer or cancerous.

Mammogram: a low dose radiation x-ray technique designed to detect changes in breast tissue which may be breast cancer.

Mastectomy:
- **Partial or segmental mastectomy**- surgery to remove the tumor and a small amount of surrounding breast tissue. Sometimes lymph nodes in the armpit are removed at the same time.
- **Total or simple mastectomy**- removal of only the breast tissue. Sometimes the lymph nodes in the

armpit are removed at the same time.
- **Modified radical mastectomy**- all the breast tissue is removed, including the lining of the chest muscle and the underarm lymph nodes.

Medical oncologist: a doctor who uses chemotherapy and hormones to treat cancer.

Metastatic: cancer that has spread to other parts of the body.

Menopause: a time in a woman's life when monthly cycles of menstruation stop forever and the level of hormones produced by the ovaries decreases.

Monoclonal antibody: a type of antibody, produced in a laboratory, which seeks out and attaches to foreign bodies, such as cancer cells.

Neo-adjuvant chemotherapy: chemotherapy given before surgery to reduce the size of a tumor.

Oncologist: a doctor who specializes in the treatment of cancer.

Oophorectomy: surgery to remove the ovaries.

Ovary: reproductive organ in the female pelvis. Ovaries are the primary source of estrogen.

Palliative treatment: therapy that relieves symptoms, such as pain does not cure the disease.

Pathologist: a doctor who examines tissue and cells under a microscope to decide if they are normal cells or cancer cells.

PET scan: a body scan that indicates areas of possible cancer activity.

Plastic and reconstructive surgeon: a doctor who can rebuild (reconstruct) a breast.

Port-a-cath: a catheter that is surgically implanted under the skin for chemotherapy infusion and blood draws.

Prognosis: a prediction about the possible outcome of a disease.

Prosthesis: an external breast form that fits into a bra after mastectomy.

Radiation oncologist: a doctor who uses radiation to treat cancer or its symptoms.

Radiologist: a doctor who reads mammograms and performs other tests such as x-rays or ultrasound.

Radiation therapy: treatment with high-energy rays to reduce the size of a cancer before surgery or to destroy and remaining cancer cells after surgery.

Reconstruction: surgery to rebuild or reconstruct a breast.

Recurrence: reappearance of cancer.

Remission: a term used to describe a decrease or disappearance of cancer for any period of time.

Risk factors: anything that increases a person's chance of developing cancer.

Screening: search for disease before there are symptoms in the hope of finding it early and at a more treatable phase. Screening includes clinical breast exam, mammography, and breast-self exam.

Second opinion: Seeking the advice of another medical doctor with similar credentials to assist in the decision-making process.

Sentinel lymph node procedure: the tumor site is injected with a blue dye and/or a radioisotope which flows to the sentinel node. This node is removed and examined by a pathologist. If there are no cancer cells in the sentinel node, no further nodes are removed.

S-phase fraction (SPF): the percentage of cells that replicate their DNA. DNA replication usually indicates that a cell is getting ready to split into two cells. A low SPF indicates a slow-growing tumor; a high SPF indicates a rapidly growing tumor.

Stage: the extent of the cancer. Stage is determined by the size of the tumor and the presence or absence of cancer cells in the lymph nodes or at other body sites.

Stem cell: immature cells in the bone marrow and blood that produce new bone marrow and blood cells.

Stereotactic: image-guided procedure that helps locate breast abnormalities and obtain tissue samples for diagnosis.

Surgeon: a doctor who performs biopsies and other surgical procedures such as removal of a lump (lumpectomy) or a breast (mastectomy).

Systemic therapy: treatment, such as chemotherapy or hormone therapy, that effects the entire body.

Tamoxifen: a hormone blocker used to treat breast cancer.

Tram Flap (Transverse Rectus Abdominus Muscle Flap): reconstruction with tissue from the stomach that replaces a breast that has been removed my mastectomy.

Tumor: an abnormal growth of cells, which are either benign or malignant.

Tumor marker: levels in the blood that are monitored to determine if cancer cells are present. An elevated level may also be caused by other conditions.

Ultrasound: an imaging technique that uses sound waves to distinguish between breast cysts and tumors.

X-rays: a type of radiation. Low doses of x-rays are used to diagnose disease; high doses of x-rays are used to treat cancer. The term is frequently used to refer to the picture created with x-rays.

Glossary terms are courtesy of Orange County Breast Cancer Coalition

Gynecologic Cancer Signs & Symptoms

Cervical Cancer
- Pelvic Pain
- Pain during intercourse
- Abnormal vaginal bleeding
- Vaginal disgorge

Ovarian Cancer
- Unusual abdominal feeling of fullness
- Pelvic discomfort
- Unexplained indigestion, gas, or bloating
- Swelling and/or pain in the abdomen

Uterine (Endometrial) Cancer
- Unusual vaginal bleeding or discharge
- Difficult or painful urination
- Pain during intercourse
- Pelvic pain

Note: It is important to know your family history. An annual gynecologic exam is recommended.
If you develop these symptoms, consult your gynecologist.

Provided by Women's Cancer Research Foundation
351 Hospital Road, Suite 506
Newport Beach, CA 92663

www.womenscancerresearchfoundation.com

Breast Cancer Signs & Symptoms

- Lump or swelling in the breast or lymph nodes under the arm
- Spontaneous nipple discharge
- Nipple turning inward that is new
- Changes in skin of nipple or breast including scaling, redness, or any change in color
- Dimpling of breast skin
- Change in shape of breast
- Non-cyclical breast pain (Does not come and go with menstrual cycle.)

Note: It is important to know your family history. An annual gynecologic exam is recommended.
If you develop these symptoms, consult your gynecologist.

Provided by Women's Cancer Research Foundation
351 Hospital Road, Suite 506
Newport Beach, CA 92663

www.womenscancerresearchfoundation.com

Also Available:

$19.95
Hardcover/ Full color book written from a child's perspective.

To order your copy(ies):

Please visit www.mycancermommy.com
or
Amazon.com

ISBN: 978-0-578-01205-6

PO Box 1442 Lake Forest, CA 92630